CW00950058

THE CHILD'S LEGAL JOURNEY THROUGH CARE

Shefali Shah

ADOPTION & FOSTERING ACADEMY

Published by
CoramBAAF Adoption and Fostering Academy
41 Brunswick Square
London WC1N 1AZ
www.corambaaf.org.uk

Coram Academy Limited, registered as a company limited by guarantee in England and Wales number 9697712, part of the Coram group, charity number 312278

British Library Cataloguing in Publication Data
A catalogue record for this book is available from the British Library

ISBN 978 1 910039 90 8

Project management by Jo Francis, Publications Department, CoramBAAF
Designed and typeset by Helen Joubert Design
Printed in Great Britain
Trade distribution by Turnaround Publisher Services, Unit 3, Olympia Trading Estate, Coburg Road, London N22 6TZ

 For the latest news on CoramBAAF titles and special offers, sign up to our free publications bulletin at https://corambaaf.org.uk/subscribe.

Contents

It is good to have an end to journey toward;
but it is the journey that matters, in the end.

Ursula K Le Guin, *The Left Hand of Darkness*

Note about the author

Shefali Shah qualified as a solicitor in 1995, and has been continuously practising since, with over 25 years' experience in child law, the majority of it as a local authority solicitor and manager. Shefali has been a member of the Law Society's Children Panel accreditation scheme since 2003. She is a legal adviser to an independent adoption agency and was formerly the legal adviser to Adoption UK and to the Independent Review Mechanism for England. She is a long-standing member of CoramBAAF's Legal Group Advisory Committee.

Shefali is also a national trainer and has taught child law academically on the undergraduate social work degree programme, the undergraduate law programme and on the postgraduate legal practice course. Through the platform of Kingsley Knight Training, Shefali has developed extensive training courses on child and social care law. She also regularly writes legal briefing notes and articles on child law. Further information can be found at www.kingsleyknight.co.uk.

Shefali's first book, *Key Changes to Family Justice*, published by CoramBAAF in 2016, continues to be a popular publication, useful for both social care professionals and lawyers. The publication is on the reading list of an academic programme for Social Work Step Up students, and is purchased by a number of local authorities to support the Assessed and Supported Year in Employment programme for newly qualified social workers.

Acknowledgements

The creation of this guide was born from a handful of training courses that I devised and regularly delivered to lawyers and social care professionals, including foster carers. The overall aim of the training was to support professionals to understand the law and its practical application to everyday social work practice.

I am grateful for all the contributions of the participants who attended these legal training sessions. Their shared experiences, observations and examples of good practice have helped to shape this guide.

I would also like to thank everyone at CoramBAAF who helped in the creation of this guide. In particular, I would like to express my gratitude to Alexandra Conroy Harris and Leonie Jordan (Legal Consultants) for finding time to read and comment on the draft. I am also immensely grateful to Shaila Shah (former Managing Director), and Jo Francis (Publishing Manager) for their immense patience and professional skill that has transformed this guide into an excellently designed publication.

A special thank you to my family for their continual support.

Note

Every effort has been made to trace and acknowledge ownership of copyright and to clear permission for material reproduced in this book. The publisher will be pleased to make suitable arrangements to clear permission with any copyright holders whom it has not been possible to contact.

The legislation and regulations detailed in this guide specifically relate to the current law in England.

Disclaimer

The contents of this guide are not intended to be relied upon as legal advice.

Introduction

The aim of this book is to be a useful, accessible guide to understanding a child's legal journey through care. There can be many reasons why a child may come into care; however, the fact that they are in care means that they are in need of support and/or safeguarding. It is therefore important that those responsible for supporting this vulnerable group of children fully understand children's rights and how these rights can be exercised. This, in turn, will help to improve the child's experience in care and assist in achieving the right outcomes for them.

There is no standard case in the child care system; each child's case will take its own journey depending on the facts, all unique to the child's particular circumstances. What is hoped is that by following the children's journeys in the principal case study provided in this guide, reading the case examples and the published case law, the reader will understand the different legal processes a child could be subject to as they pass through the various legal stages before and during the local authority's involvement. The guide will outline what statutory services the child can be entitled to and the local authority's responsibilities to the child during their journey in care.

The guide can be used as a resource for those working with children, foster carers, prospective adopters, social care professionals, social workers, youth workers, teachers, CAFCASS officers, and members of the legal profession. The guide's aim is to support those honourable professionals who undertake the invaluable and immense task of protecting, advocating and care planning for this group of vulnerable children and young people every day. The guide can also be of assistance to children's carers, parents, those who are supporting parents, and, of course, the child or young person themselves.

To all of those reading this guide, I sincerely hope it supports you to understand the law and appreciate how it can be applied in practice. Arming yourself with up-to-date knowledge will in turn assist you in supporting the children and young people you are responsible for through their journey in care and beyond, a journey that will also have an impact into their adulthood.

Case studies

The case examples cited in the guide are real-life cases of which I have personally had conduct. I have included these to highlight points and demonstrate the application of the law and good practice.

Note: The events described in the cases where I have had conduct have been based on memories of my experiences as the solicitor with conduct of the case. The identifying features of the people, locations and/or events have been changed, modified or merged in order to protect the privacy and identity of the children, families and professionals. Any likenesses, resemblance or similarities are purely unintentional and/or coincidental.

The names and facts of the principal Lesland case study, that tracks the journey of three children through the care system, are fictitious.

Case study 1: A life's journey

This case follows a young girl's journey through care and demonstrates how the right support can make significant changes and help to turn an early tragedy into a future successful journey. Success stories in this field are rarely shared or celebrated and, in my view, should be, in order to highlight the impact that support can have on a child's journey and life.

This is a historic case. Sarah, aged 10, was placed in local authority care with her brother, James, after being found to have suffered sexual abuse by her birth father whilst living at home. The parents agreed for both children to be placed in foster care.

After the children had been in foster carer for about 8 months, the father passed away. The mother agreed to be reassessed and it was agreed by children's services that Sarah could be returned to her care. James had learning disabilities and the mother agreed that he should remain in foster care. Sarah returned home and regular contact was set up between the children's mother, Sarah and James.

The local authority commenced care proceedings in respect of James and at the end of the proceedings was granted a care order. James' care plan was for him to remain in long-term foster care.

The children's mother then formed a relationship with another man, Frank. Shortly after commencing this new relationship, Frank moved into the family home. Whilst living there, Frank sexually abused Sarah. Sarah made disclosures to her teacher. Her mother refused to end her relationship with Frank and, with her agreement, Sarah was brought back into foster care.

Sarah was now 13 years old. She was placed in a different foster placement to James and continued to have regular sibling contact. The local authority applied for and was granted a care order in respect of Sarah, and she had supervised contact with her mother.

By the time Sarah turned 16, her mother no longer maintained contact with her or James. Sarah had developed a relationship with a man called David, who was aged 35. Sarah stated that she was in love with David, and both Sarah and David wanted to be in a committed relationship with each other. The concern for the local authority was that David was nearly 20 years older than Sarah, and that Sarah was extremely vulnerable due to her past history of abuse. Sarah informed her social worker, Abigail, that if she was not permitted to see David, she would run away from her foster placement.

Both David and Sarah stated that they would co-operate with any conditions that Abigail wanted to place on their relationship, as long as they could see each other. Abigail, in consultation with her manager, was of the view that if Sarah was not supported in maintaining her relationship with David in a safe way, it would in fact place Sarah at greater risk as she was likely to "vote with her feet" and run away.

It was agreed that the only way of safeguarding Sarah was to support her and to place conditions on how and when she and David could meet. Sarah agreed to remain in foster care until she was 18 years old. For two years, both Sarah and David kept to the conditions imposed on them as part of a safety agreement and maintained their relationship. At age 18, with Abigail's and the local authority's knowledge and support, Sarah moved in with David and, shortly after, they were married.

Abigail remained at the same local authority and was initially promoted to team manager and then service manager.

Despite the fact that Abigail was no longer a frontline social worker, and nor was she Sarah's worker, every time Sarah had a significant event she would notify Abigail. When she gave birth to a child, Sarah sent Abigail a card with a photo of the baby; in the card, she gave an update about the progress of her life. Despite leaving care and being an adult, Sarah still considered Abigail to be part of her connected network of support. Each time the correspondence was received, Abigail would place it in Sarah's social care file held by the local authority.

Ten years after leaving care, Sarah requested access to her file, and this is when I became involved in the case. Abigail was now a service manager; she brought the file to the legal department and requested that I check it, as an application had been made by Sarah to access her records. I checked the file for third party information, duly redacted non-disclosable information, and thereafter the information was made available to Sarah. I saw the photos of each of Sarah's beautiful babies. I subsequently left the employment of this local authority.

Fifteen years after leaving this post, I was asked to deliver some legal training to an independent fostering provider (IFP). When I arrived on the day of the training, I was pleasantly surprised to meet Abigail, who now worked for the IFP. We discussed our past employment with the same local authority, and as part of those discussions, Sarah's case came up. I stated that I was so impressed that Sarah always considered Abigail as her social worker even after leaving care, not just for her minority, but for life.

Abigail stated that 25 years after leaving care, Sarah needed help to locate her brother, James, with whom she had lost touch. In her search, the first person Sarah contacted was Abigail, whom she tracked down at the IFP. Sarah still considered Abigail to be part of her support network after all these years. Sarah, who was now in her 40s, informed Abigail that she was still married to David, and they were still together. Sadly, David had developed dementia and Sarah was now also his carer. Sarah explained that their children were grown up and she and David lived in a small close-knit village. She told Abigail that if it had not been for her support when she was in care and after she left, she was not sure if she would have had such a successful adult life and a happy marriage.

I was honoured that I had come to know about Sarah's journey in care and in adulthood. Sarah had greatly benefited from a social worker who had used her judgement to support Sarah in her wishes, balancing this with ensuring that there was a framework that enabled her to be protected. Abigail's input had helped shape Sarah's life journey successfully.

___

1

The legal framework

The UK has created one of the most advanced and successful child protection systems in the world, developed from many decades of reforms. One of the ways in which this success is measured is that, since the 1980s, the UK has seen the lowest rate of child abuse-related deaths compared to other major developed countries (Pritchard and Williams, 2009). This is combined with a child protection system that incorporates a host of well-established legislation and guidance protecting children's rights and welfare.

The safeguarding of children is now considered to be everyone's responsibility, meaning that all organisations have a duty to safeguard and promote the welfare of children. The legislative framework sets out the steps to be undertaken by children's services departments for the protection of children. Safeguarding is defined by the statutory guidance *Working Together to Safeguard Children* (Department for Education (DfE), 2018, p 102) as:

1. Protecting children from maltreatment

2. Preventing impairment of children's health or development

3. Ensuring that children are growing up in circumstances consistent with the provision of safe and effective care

4. Taking action to enable all children to have the best outcomes

Child protection is part of safeguarding and the promotion of the child's welfare. These powers are granted by Parliament to local authorities by statute. Local authorities are considered to be "creatures of statute", meaning that they themselves were created by statute. For that reason, local authorities are unable to act beyond the powers granted to them by Parliament.

The Local Authority Social Services Act 1970 created a framework that required every local authority to establish a social services department to carry out social service functions, including the provision of support for families. This Act was seen as a significant shift towards creating a co-ordinated and comprehensive approach to not only support families but also encourage people to seek assistance from the local authority. This is true even today, local authority social services departments can and do provide support to families, within their statutory powers, should this be considered necessary. This can be in the form of signposting, giving advice or providing direct assistance.

Since the passing of the 1970 Act, there have been many reforms, all intended to improve child protection processes, many of which will be explored in this guide.

Legislation and regulations are important as they support the creation of a single and unified code of practice; however, they alone cannot provide for a complete child protection system. As noted by Professor Eileen Munro, 'A good child protection system should be concerned with the child's journey through the system from needing to receiving help, keeping a clear focus on children's best interests throughout' (2011).

It also requires the ability for flexible professional judgement. Professor Eileen Munro identified in her reports (2010 and 2011) how over-regulation of processes can get in the way of social workers using their discretion and judgement to enable them to build meaningful relationships with children, prioritise children's needs, and take action without delay. Therefore, for the operation of a successful child protection system, there needs to be a fine balance between regulating children's services and having a system that permits professionals and, in particular, social workers to take action in accordance with the child's needs and, if possible, to act on their wishes. It is therefore essential that processes are continuously evaluated and fine-tuned, resulting in the development of a child welfare system that is dynamic and capable of adapting in accordance with the needs of society. This, combined with a continuum of improving practices and processes, helps to create an environment that has the function and ability to facilitate the best outcomes for children.

One of the ways in which the child protection system can be improved and refined is to consider its practical functioning. This is unfortunately at times undertaken when there is a child death as a result of abuse. One significant positive outcome from these tragic cases is the professional learning from Inquiries and serious case reviews (SCR)[1] that has helped to identify failings in the system. This learning then leads to active steps being undertaken to improve practice, with the hope that a potentially harmful situation will be identified prior to another child being at risk of significant harm.

The learning can even have national implications. For example, the death of Victoria Climbié in 2000 led to the introduction of major changes, including implementation of the Children Act 2004. Victoria, an eight-year-old child from the Ivory Coast who was brought to the UK by her relative, died after being subjected to torture and inhumane treatment by her carers. Victoria's tragic death resulted in a Public Inquiry, chaired by Lord Laming, which on its conclusion resulted in significant changes to the law and practice. The Inquiry (Laming, 2003) made a staggering 108 recommendations to improve the child protection system. It also contributed to the then Government's introduction of the Every Child Matters reforms (HM Government, 2003), designed to improve early intervention by expanding the contribution of all services involved with children and their families. Parliament also passed the Children Act 2004 to improve children's services and promote early intervention. This Act supplemented the Children Act 1989, taking a child-centred approach and reinforcing the message that safeguarding and promoting children's welfare are the responsibility of all organisations and agencies working with children.

The 2004 Act also required local authorities to replace Area Child Protection Committees (ACPC) with the establishment of Local Safeguarding Children's Boards (LSCB). Both ACPCs and LSCBs had representatives from multiple agencies and professionals responsible for safeguarding children in their local area. The main difference between the two was that LSCBs had a statutory footing and wider focus, introducing the key principle that safeguarding children

---

1   From June 2018, serious case reviews have been replaced by child safeguarding practice reviews introduced by the Children and Social Work Act 2017. This new panel's role is to identify improvements to be made in order to promote children's welfare.

in the local authority's area is the responsibility of any professional, that is, anyone who comes into contact with a child (Working Together, 2018, p 10, para 16) and not just that of statutory agencies. The local authority continues to have lead responsibility.

As a result of the continual evolving process, the Children and Social Work Act 2017 replaced LSCBs,[2] as they were not considered to be sufficiently effective, with new local arrangements working with Safeguarding Partners, that is, the local authority, police and health. The partners are required to work together to identify and respond to children's needs in their area.

As can be seen, the tragic death of Victoria Climbié triggered a chain of changes resulting in reforms designed to strengthen child protection processes and improve the effective safeguarding and welfare of children.

The continual improvement of matters relating to children and young people is also demonstrated by the flow of Acts of Parliament. The key legislation relating to the welfare of children is the Children Act 1989, which is supported by a number of later statutes that impact on the welfare of children and young people.

These are as follows:

- Children (Leaving Care) Act 2000
- Adoption and Children Act 2002
- Children Act 2004
- Children and Adoption Act 2006
- Children and Young Persons Act 2008
- Children and Families Act 2014
- Children and Social Work Act 2017

Other legislation that also impacts on children and young people includes:

- Mental Health Act 1983

2   S.30 Children and Social Work Act 2017 amends ss.13–16 Children Act 2004.

- Human Rights Act 1998

- Mental Capacity Act 2005

- Equality Act 2010

- Care Act 2014

- Data Protection Act 2018

This guide explores the major aspects of the significant legislation, statutory guidance and case law when following the child's legal journey.

We have already discussed that the law cannot undertake the vast task of safeguarding and promoting children's welfare alone, it also requires sound professional judgement and the ability of professionals to work in a collaborative multi-agency forum within a framework of effective systems and processes, thereby enabling sustainable and positive outcomes for children and ensuring that safeguarding children remains a shared responsibility. This process is supported by s.27 of the Children Act 1989, which requires co-operation between authorities, together with s.10 and s.11 of the Children Act 2004, which require each local authority to make arrangements to promote co-operation between the authority's relevant partners, persons or bodies to improve the well-being of children in the authority's area, including protection from harm and neglect.

1   Childhood

A child is defined in the Children Act 1989 as any young person under the age of 18[3] (the age of majority) and childhood begins from the moment the child is born. A child will gain certain rights as they grow older and before they are 18; however, in law, irrespective of how mature the child is, they will remain a child until they reach 18, when in law they are then recognised as an adult.

In English law, the unborn child – that is, the foetus – is not recognised as a person and the law is unable to override the mother's rights whilst the child is in

---

3   S.105(1) Children Act 1989

utero. This was highlighted in *Re F (In Utero)*,[4] where the local authority applied to protect the safety of an unborn child due to concerns about the mother, who suffered from mental health problems and had abused drugs. The Court of Appeal ruled that the court did not have any jurisdiction over the unborn child and that the child could only be protected once born, as to do so beforehand would give the court inappropriate control over the mother's life and, effectively, her body. Therefore, all the legislation relating to children is only applicable once the child is born, and no legal proceedings can be commenced until that day.

A child who is looked after is one who is provided with accommodation for a continuous period of more than 24 hours, and is:

- accommodated under s.20 of the Children Act 1989;

- subject to a voluntary arrangement between the local authority and parents with parental responsibility (a concept that is discussed later);

- subject to a care order (s.31 Children Act 1989) or interim care order (s.38 Children Act 1989);

- subject to a placement order with a care plan of being placed for adoption (s.21 Adoption and Children Act 2002).

Children who have been looked after by the local authority, subject to meeting the criteria (explained later in this guide), may be entitled to services from the local authority, post their 18th birthday, under leaving care services. These services are provided to eligible care leavers to give them the same level of care and support that children who are not in care would reasonably expect to receive from their parents or carers to enable them to transition smoothly into adulthood. If the child who was looked after is eligible for leaving care services, at 18 their status will change to that of a young adult, receiving advice and assistance under the Children (Leaving Care) Act 2000. Also at 18, now as young adults, their social worker and care plan are replaced with the allocation of a personal adviser from the leaving care team, and a pathway plan. This pathway plan will detail the services and support that the young person will require from the age of 18.

4   *Re F (In Utero)* [1998] Fam 122

The assessment of the pathway plan is undertaken by the social worker and the personal adviser prior to the child's 18th birthday.

The planning for adulthood for a child who is in care should start as early as possible, and for some local authorities this could be as early as when the child reaches the age of 14, with advice and support from the social worker and/or the child's foster carer in learning tasks such as cooking, cleaning and budgeting. This early process helps the social worker to start supporting the child in their transition to adulthood, and to consider how best to support the child's aspirations and goals in relation to all aspects of their life, including education, training or employment that the child wishes to pursue.

Good practice requires that local authorities should introduce the child, no later than their 16th birthday, to their allocated personal adviser, who will then work closely with the child's social worker until they take over when the child is 18. This ensures that the child begins to develop a relationship with the personal adviser, whilst still receiving support from their social worker, making the transfer of support easier for the young person to manage.

2 International conventions

2.1 Human rights

Human rights are the basic rights that safeguard the fundamental freedoms of everyone in the UK. The European Convention on Human Rights and Fundamental Freedoms, often referred to in short as the European Convention on Human Rights (ECHR), came into force in September 1953. The Convention is a series of Articles that set out the civil rights that all citizens of signatory states are entitled to. The UK Government ratified the ECHR, which means that UK citizens have its protection and can bring an action for breach of their human rights. Although the ECHR is written post-World War II, it stays relevant and alive for today's society as it is treated as a living instrument that will be interpreted in light of present-day changes in society and family life (*Tyrer v United Kingdom*).[5] This process was

---

5   *Tyrer v United Kingdom* [1978] 2 EHRR 1, [1978] ECHR 20

simplified with the passing of the Human Rights Act 1998,[6] which incorporated the EHCR rights and freedoms into domestic British law and permitted complainants to now bring an action against public bodies to the UK courts. If the case cannot be resolved in the UK courts, it can still proceed on appeal to the European Court of Human Rights, based in Strasbourg, France.

Protection of human rights is available to both adults and children, on the basis that children are humans entitled to protection (Fortin, 2009, p 33). The ECHR is now nearly 70 years old, and the language can appear quite outdated.

Prior to the UK leaving the European Union (EU) on 31 January 2020, famously known as Brexit, the Government gave a commitment to its continued ECHR membership (HM Government, July 2018), *The Future Relationship between the United Kingdom and the European Union*). This was confirmed again on 5 March 2020 when, in response to media enquiries, Downing Street announced that 'the UK is committed to the European Convention on Human Rights and to protecting human rights and championing them at home and abroad' (*The Independent*).

The actions and decisions of local authorities, as public bodies with responsibilities for children's social care, must be compatible with human rights requirements. Children's services, whether provided by the local authority or on its behalf, have a statutory obligation to treat children and families in accordance with their human rights. Local authorities must ensure that everyone is treated with dignity, respect, fairness, and that the child or their family members are able to exercise their rights and for their views to be considered in any decision-making process. When considering any policies, actions or decisions, there may be interference with a child's or family's human rights, and in such cases, the local authority must be satisfied that the interference is necessary and proportionate, for example, to safeguard a child.

There are 16 basic human rights. The Articles in the ECHR are categorised in three different types; that is, absolute, qualified and limited rights. Absolute rights are those that the local authority must adhere to and cannot depart from or restrict its obligations. Article 3 falls under this category. Qualified rights can be restricted in certain circumstances where a local authority is entitled to interfere in these

6   The Human Rights Act 1998 came into force in the UK in October 2000.

13

rights. Article 8 is a qualified right; that is, the local authority can legitimately interfere in family life if it is proportionate and necessary to safeguard a child's welfare. Limited rights have a limited scope; Article 6 is an example of a limited right. These articles are discussed in further detail below.

For the purposes of this guide, the key articles that regularly impact on social care cases are as follows:

- **Article 3: Freedom from torture and inhuman or degrading treatment**
  No one has the right to inflict torture, inhuman or degrading treatment on anyone and any attempt to do so is incompatible with this right. Inhuman treatment can include serious physical assault, serious physical or psychological abuse, and/or threatening to torture someone. This right is an "absolute right", meaning it cannot be restricted or limited in any way.

  A v United Kingdom[7] is an illustration of the impact of the application of Article 3 in child protection matters. An eight-year-old boy, A, admittedly very badly behaved, was caned by his stepfather, F, on numerous occasions. F was charged under s.47 of the Offences Against the Person Act 1861 for assault causing actual bodily harm. During the trial, F successfully claimed the English law defence that A's beating was reasonable chastisement, and he was acquitted.

  The case went before the European Court of Human Rights, brought on behalf of the child against the State (UK Government), that the English law relating to lawful chastisement failed to protect A and violated A's Article 3 rights.

  The European Court held that the caning did reach a level of severity prohibited by Article 3 rights; that is, A should not have been subjected to inhuman or degrading treatment. Allowing F to rely on the defence meant that it was the UK Government that had violated A's Article 3 rights by failing to provide A with adequate protection under the English law relating to chastisement. The court took the view that there was a positive responsibility on the UK Government to take effective measures to prevent conduct that would come within this Article.

---

7   *A v United Kingdom* [1998] 2 FLR 959, Times 1/10/98, ECHR

- **Article 5: Right to liberty and security**

  Everyone has the right not to be deprived of their liberty except in limited cases specified in the Article (for example, when suspected or convicted of committing a crime, and provided there is proper basis in UK law for their arrest or detention). This Article will be particularly relevant in cases where the local authority is considering deprivation of a child's liberty. This is a limited right and can be lawfully restricted, which means that a young person's liberty can be lawfully deprived if authorised by statute or common law.

  A child's liberty can be deprived in a number of ways:

  - With the granting of a secure accommodation order under s.25 of the Children Act 1989. This order authorises the child to be placed in secure accommodation and thereby restricts their liberty. The criteria for the application of this order are where the child is likely to injure themselves or others, or abscond and therefore place themself at risk of significant harm.

  - Under the Mental Health Act 1983, for the purposes of admission and treatment of a child's mental disorder in a hospital.

  - The Mental Capacity Act 2005 makes it lawful to deprive a child of 16 and over of their liberty when they lack capacity to consent to the care that they are receiving, including where they live and how they are cared for on a day-to-day basis. This can include foster care or a residential placement, and where it is necessary so as to sustain their life or prevent serious deterioration.

  - Youth remand, youth detention accommodation or local authority accommodation under the Legal Aid, Sentencing and Punishment of Offenders Act 2012.

  - Criminal sentencing provisions of the Power of Criminal Courts (Sentencing) Act 2000.

  - Deprivation of liberty for children under 16 can be authorised in the exercise of the inherent jurisdiction of the High Court.

- **Article 6: Right to a fair trial**

  Everyone, including children, has the right to a fair and public hearing within a reasonable period of time. When care proceedings have commenced, all parties will be entitled to legal representation. This includes children who, in public law proceedings, are not only the subject of the proceedings but are also parties. Therefore, a children's solicitor is appointed to represent the child in public law proceedings. However, as children lack capacity to conduct proceedings due to their age, a Children's Guardian is appointed to give instructions to the children's solicitor on behalf of the child. The Children's Guardian is appointed by the court, is independent, and comes from the Children and Family Court Advisory and Support Service (CAFCASS). Their role is to seek the child's views and represent them in the care proceedings, and ensure that the child's welfare is promoted.

  It should be noted that for social care professionals, Article 6 rights are not just restricted to legal proceedings or where legal proceedings are being considered. This right is also applicable when working with families prior to the commencement of any legal proceedings. This requires the social workers to work in a way that is both fair and transparent in the decision-making, ensuring that the child and family members are provided with a reasoned decision within a reasonable timescale. The issue of delay can become relevant under this Article as delay can be prejudicial and considered unfair. Having a reasoned decision within a reasonable timeframe enables the child and family members to understand the basis for the decision and thereafter to consider whether they wish to challenge it. During this process, the local authority must take into account any imbalance of power and, if this is present, ensure that steps are taken to address the imbalance by providing sufficient support necessary to the child and family. In the case of Re G,[8] the local authority was criticised for failing to involve the parents properly in the decision-making process relating to changes to the children's care plans. The Judge elaborated that the local authority had a duty to provide full and frank disclosure of documents, including notes and minutes of conversations and meetings, and listed the following as important:

8   Re G (Care: Challenge to Local Authority's Decision) [2003] 2 FLR 42

- – informing the parents promptly of its plans;

- – giving factual reasons;

- – providing an opportunity for parents to answer allegations;

- – providing an opportunity to make representations; and

- – parents should have the chance to attend and address any crucial meetings.

● **Article 8: Respect for family life**

Everyone has the right for their private and family life to be respected, and this includes their home and correspondence. This right is often incorrectly referred to as the right to family life, but it is in fact a right to respect for family life. This is not an absolute right and can be restricted in specified circumstances.

A local authority can interfere in a child or family's Article 8 rights, provided that this is permitted by the law, is necessary, and is a proportionate action to the risk posed to the child's welfare. Hence, any involvement by children's services in a child's life will engage Article 8 rights, and the involvement will be an interference in the parent's and child's private and family life. Therefore, any action undertaken by the authority must be considered in light of the Article 8 rights of everyone who will be affected by this intervention, and it must be a proportionate response to the level of risk posed to the child. In *Re O*, a Court of Appeal case,[9] the appeal concerned whether the court was correct in granting a supervision order and not a care order. The Judge stated that 'the proportionality is key...as a response to the risk presented'.[10]

Social care professionals must always give due consideration to these key human rights, principles and duties. Failure to do so can place the local authority at risk of human rights challenges in court. A case that highlighted this was *Re (G) v Nottingham City Council*.[11] This case was of particular interest

---

9   *Re O (A Child) (Supervision Order: Future Harm)* [2001] EWCA Civ 16

10   *Re O (A Child) (Supervision Order: Future Harm)* [2001] EWCA Civ 16, para 28

11   *Re (G) v Nottingham City Council* [2008] EWHC 152 (Admin)

due to the publicity it received from the media. The mother, a young care leaver, gave birth to her child. The pre-birth plan was to remove the child at birth from the mother's care. When the baby was born, the baby was removed from the mother's care without an order or the mother's valid consent. The mother challenged the unlawful separation. The court found in her favour and that there had been a breach of the mother's Article 8 rights.

The appointment of a CAFCASS officer in Children Act public and sometimes private law proceedings (discussed in greater detail later in the guide) is another way in which the child's Article 8 rights are promoted.

In practice, when considering human rights issues, professionals need to be aware of the power imbalance that exists between the local authority and the parents or carers and the child. The local authority is more powerful as it has statutory powers, and when working with parents or carers, professionals should always consider ways in which to redress the power imbalance.

Social care professionals do not generally have a very good public relations image, mainly as their work is not fully understood by the public, or the profession is linked with failures in high profile child protection cases, such as the death of Baby P (Peter Connelly). In the majority of cases, instead of being welcomed into a family's life, a social worker may in fact be feared in the mistaken belief that they have the power to take a child into care, who ultimately could be adopted. Such fear and mistrust undermine public confidence in the profession and can have the impact of placing the child at greater risk. This is because instead of requesting support, the parent may be fearful of doing so due to the incorrectly held belief that, once a social worker becomes involved in the family's life, their child could be removed. Although social workers do have extensive statutory powers, what is often forgotten is that these powers can and will only be exercised if fully supported by evidence. The removal of a child from their parents' care can only be justified if the child has suffered significant harm or if their welfare is at risk of significant harm, and a decision on this is made by the courts. If there is supporting evidence, this clearly puts the social worker in a powerful position. If action is required, then the social worker must ensure that any action is necessary and proportionate to the concerns.

This imbalance of power must be addressed immediately. For example, if there are issues in relation to language or disability, sufficient support should be identified and provided from the outset by the local authority, for example, the provision of an advocate or interpreter, or the parents should be advised to seek independent legal advice or representation. The social worker must ensure that any communication with the parents or carers is fully understood so that the parent or carer can then consider what action is being proposed, the reasons for this and what steps could be taken if they do not co-operate.

Case study 2: The impact of social work intervention

A referral from a neighbour was received by children' services. The concerns were about the care of two children by their parents, who lived at 15 Summer Avenue, and the referral detailed that the children were being abused by their parents. The referral was allocated to the duty social worker. The children's names were not provided by the person making the referral. All that was known was that there were two children aged around nine and ten years old. The duty social worker planned to visit the address and ascertain more information from the parents. The social worker mistakenly noted the address and incorrectly visited 15 Summer Street, instead of 15 Summer Avenue.

When the social worker visited, she found a family with two children (of similar ages to those stated in the referral) living there. The parents were informed that concerns had been raised in relation to their care of the children. The parents did not question the social worker's visit, which they could have done in the exercise of their Article 6 rights. They fully co-operated with the social worker in her enquiries, listened attentively and agreed to do whatever she asked of them.

Following the second visit, the social worker realised that she had been visiting the wrong address and should have been visiting 15 Summer Avenue. On realising the error, she attended a third time at 15 Summer Street, this time with her team manager, and they informed the parents of the mistake. They advised the parents of their right to make a formal complaint. The involvement by children's services had interfered with this family's Article 8 rights and the parents would have been entitled to raise a valid complaint for this breach. The parents were asked why they had not questioned the social worker at the initial and subsequent visits. The parents responded that from the time the social worker first arrived at their house, they were fearful that their children could be taken into care. For that reason, they felt that they had no choice but to fully co-operate. The parents were relieved that children's services would be ending its involvement with their family. They further stated that they would not be making any complaint as this would prolong involvement with children's services.

The parents' reaction is not surprising; they felt powerless when the social worker's investigation commenced. Understandably, they were extremely grateful when the social worker and team manager were ready to leave, after receiving confirmation that the case file would be closed with no further action.

Before closing such a case, it is good practice that the local authority should inform and agree with the parents what, if any, records will be retained by children's services, and provide written details of the parents' right to make a complaint.

2.2   Conflict of rights: children v parents

As detailed above, both children and adults have the right to the protection of their human rights. What if there is a conflict between the child's rights and the parents' rights? Whose rights take precedence? The ECHR has clearly established that where there is conflict, the child's best interests will prevail. The ECHR in *Johansen v Norway*[12] held that, in carrying out this balancing exercise:[13]

The court will attach particular importance to the best interests of the child which, depending on their nature and seriousness, may override those of the parent. In particular the parent cannot be entitled under Article 8 of the ECHR to have such measures taken as would harm the child's health and development.[14]

12   *Johansen v Norway* [1997] 23 EHRR 3
13   Johansen v Norway [1997] 23 EHRR 33, para 78
14   *Johansen v Norway* [1996] 23 EHRR 33, para 78

In a subsequent decision in *Yousef v Netherlands*,[15] the ECHR reiterated:

> *...that in judicial decisions where the rights under Article 8 of parents and those of a child are at stake, the child's rights must be the paramount consideration. If any balancing of interests is necessary, the interests of the child must prevail.*[16]

The Yousef case followed the approach taken in the earlier ECHR case of *Johansen v Norway*.[17]

A similar approach was taken in a later ECHR case of *Gurgulu v Germany*.[18] In this case, a father discovered the existence of his child three months after the child's birth; at four days old, the child had been placed with prospective adopters. The father sought for the child to be placed in his care but was unsuccessful, on the basis of the child having established a relationship with the prospective adopters, which it would not be in the child's best interests to sever. The father did, however, establish a violation of his Article 8 rights before the ECHR which applied the Johansen test, on the basis that the domestic courts had not sufficiently explored all possible solutions to the problem:

> *Article 8 requires that the domestic authorities should strike a fair balance between the interests of the child and those of the parents and that, in the balancing process, particular importance should be attached to the best interests of the child which, depending on their nature and seriousness, may override those of the parents.*[19]

2.3 United Nations Convention on the Rights of the Child

An important international human rights treaty in relation to children's rights is the United Nations Convention on the Rights of the Child (UNCRC). Adopted by the United Nations on 20 November 1989 and ratified by the UK Government in

15 *Yousef v Netherlands* (Application no. 33711/96) 2002
16 *Yousef v Netherlands* (Application no. 33711/96) 2002, para 73
17 *Johansen v Norway* [1996] 23 EHRR 33
18 *Gurgulu v Germany* [2004] 1 FLR 894
19 *Gurgulu v Germany* [2004] 1 FLR 894, para 43

December 1991, it requires the UK Government to make laws, policies and practice fully compatible with this Convention.

The Convention has 54 articles, covering all aspects of a child's life, including their civil, political, economic, social and cultural rights. The Convention is to be considered as a whole, with no individual right more important or influential than another, and all being interrelated. All the rights in the Convention apply equally to all children (Article 2), and the best interests of the child shall be a primary consideration in all actions concerning children (Article 3).

3 Domestic law

3.1 Children Act 1989

The Children Act 1989 was drafted to be consistent with the UNCRC. It created a single coherent legal framework encompassing all previously existing welfare legislation pertaining to children (with the exception of criminal legislation) into one piece of legislation dealing with both private and public law proceedings. At the time of its passing, it was considered progressive and radical, as not only did it produce an umbrella enactment providing a comprehensive and consistent legal framework in child law, but it also introduced a fundamental change of approach by the courts and professionals involved in children's cases.

When the Bill was introduced to Parliament, Lord Mackay described it as:

> ...the most comprehensive and far reaching reform of child law which has come before Parliament in living memory.[20]

The legislation's main aims were the subject of parliamentary discussions before its enactment, and clarified as such:

> The Children Bill has two main aims. The first is to gather together in one place...one coherent whole, all the law relating to care and upbringing of children and the provision of social services for them. The second is to provide a consistent set of legal remedies which will be available

20 HL Deb 06 December 1988 vol 502 cc487–540

in all courts and in all proceedings. Such simple aims should not be as
revolutionary as, in fact, they are.[21]

Even today, the Children Act 1989 remains the most important piece of legislation concerning children's welfare. Any relevant changes introduced in subsequent legislation are incorporated into this Act, thereby making it relevant and current to today's children and families.

The Children Act celebrated 30 years of its existence on 12 April 2019. Sir Andrew McFarlane, President of the Family Division, in his speech at the Nicolas Wall Memorial Lecture, stated:

The Children Act was groundbreaking to a very high level...it changed the
work of children law and it has...stood the test of time...The architects of the
legislation, and its draftsman, simply got it right...and [it] continues to be
to the great benefit of the children and young people whose needs it was
aimed to meet.[22]

The Act aims to promote and safeguard the welfare of children, enabling them to be brought up within their family wherever possible. It starts from the premise that the best place for a child is with their family:

The 1989 Act rests on the belief that children are generally best looked after
within the family with both parents playing a full part and without resort
to legal proceedings. That belief is reflected in the new concept of parental
responsibility...the local authority's duty to give support for children and
their families...the local authority's duty to return a child looked after by
them to his family unless this is against his interests.

(Department of Health, 1989, p 1, para 1.4)

This principle of maintaining the child within the family is also enshrined in Article 7 of the UNCRC, and the local authority's duty to safeguard and promote children's welfare set out in s.17 of the Children Act 1989. However, this principle needs to be balanced with the child's right for protection from abuse and neglect.

21   HC Deb 26 October 1989 vol 158 cc1074–118
22   The lecture was presented on 9 May 2019.

Therefore, the success of any child protection system requires it to be child-centred, recognising parents' rights and acknowledging that children also have rights.

3.2   Recognition of children's rights

Children's rights is not a new concept, and in fact can be traced from the late 1700s and has been developing since the 1800s. The Victorians passed a number of laws protecting children's well-being at work, school and in the home. However, these reforms must be understood alongside the Victorian view of children's rights, which was defined in relation to their future role as citizens. This period adopted a paternalistic approach, seeing the child as the property of the father, with the father taking the responsibility of making all decisions for his child. Prince Albert (Queen Victoria's husband) reflected this view when he argued that the working man's children were 'part of his productive power', an indispensable source of family income (Horn, 1997a, 1997b).

Moving on from the Victorian era, there began an encouraging progression and gradual shift from parental rights to acknowledging the need to safeguard children's welfare. This then progressed to recognising that children's legal rights are separate to those of their parents, with a need to treat children as individuals rather than to categorise them as a collective and undifferentiated class (Freeman, 2007). This progression led to an advancement of the protection of children, resulting in the introduction of legislation relating to children's education and welfare. This was further supported with the creation of national children's charities such as Barnardo's in 1867 and the NSPCC in 1884, whose aim was to protect children. Implementation of legislation also assisted to further this transformation, such as the enactment of the Prevention of Cruelty to, and Protection of, Children Act 1889, which for the first time enabled the State to intervene in the prevention of cruelty to children.

Fast forwarding to the implementation of the Children Act 1989, this further enhanced the concept of children's rights by shifting the focus away from parental rights to the recognition of parental responsibility, acknowledging that children are not their parents' property or to be protected only by charities. The

Children Act 1989 supported children's rights by introducing key principles, the first recognises that the child's welfare is of paramount importance in all decisions and introduces the "welfare checklist",[23] a list of factors to be considered in determining the child's best interests. Whenever the court has to consider any question in relation to the upbringing of a child, the court will apply the welfare checklist as set out in s.1(3) of the Children Act 1989:

A court shall have regard in particular to—

(a) the ascertainable wishes and feelings of the child concerned (considered in the light of his age and understanding);

(b) his physical, emotional and educational needs;

(c) the likely effect on him of any change in his circumstances;

(d) his age, sex, background and any characteristics of his which the court considers relevant;

(e) any harm which he has suffered or is at risk of suffering;

(f) how capable each of his parents, and any other person in relation to whom the court considers the question to be relevant, is of meeting his needs;

(g) the range of powers available to the court under this Act in the proceedings in question.

The checklist does not detail race, religion, language or culture, and if these factors relating to the child need to be highlighted, then they can be referred to in the welfare checklist under paragraph (d).

To assist the court in considering what is in the child's best interests, statements or reports provided to the court by social workers or children's guardians when dealing with matters concerning the child's welfare must include the welfare checklist in relation to each child.

23 S.1(3) Children Act 1989

The Children Act 1989 also introduced the concept of parental responsibility,[24] reflecting the then Parliament's view that parenthood was a matter of responsibility and not just rights. Lord Laming recognised that parenthood is a lifetime commitment (2010, p 7); however, legal rights over one's child are not.

At the same time as the Children Act 1989 was being shaped in the late 1980s, there were developments in the recognition of the rights-based approach to children, which influenced the drafting of the Act. The key areas were:

- the development of human rights issues;

- the Cleveland Report (Butler-Sloss, 1988), which examined the inappropriate handling by professionals of the removal of a large number of children from their homes in Cleveland in 1987, without sufficient evidence to support that they were at risk of or had suffered sexual abuse; and

- the Gillick Case,[25] which established that a child who has capacity and maturity can consent to medical decisions without parental permission or even knowledge. It also firmly recognised the child or young person's right to make decisions about themselves, in accordance with their evolving capacity of understanding.

Each of these points, in their own way, created a wave of change leading to a marked transition from a paternalistic approach to recognising the child as a separate legal entity with rights similar to adult rights, and children not simply being regarded as "objects of concern" (Butler-Sloss, 1988). The Children Act 1989 did not eradicate the concept of parental rights but achieved a fine balance with recognition of the evolving rights of children. This was an important shift as it resulted in improvement of the treatment of children (Ferguson, 2013, p 188) and signalled that children deserve equal respect (p 184). The Children Act 1989 achieved this by being child-centred and focusing on children's needs. It recognised that children, like adults, should also have a voice with a right to express themselves and if unable or too young to do so directly, that their best interests need to be represented.

---

24 S.2 Children Act 1989

25 *Gillick v West Norfolk & Wisbeck Area Health Authority* [1986] AC 112 House of Lords

At the time of its implementation in October 1991, the Children Act 1989 introduced a number of other key fundamental principles that run like a golden thread through the whole of the Act and apply to both private and public law children proceedings, which are explored in the next section.

3.3   Key principles of the Children Act 1989

Paramountcy principle

As discussed, the Act introduced a balance between the parents' rights to exercise their legal responsibilities (known as parental responsibility) towards their children, alongside the State's (that is, the local authority's) duty to intervene where the child's welfare requires protection. Section 1(1) of the Act states that the child's welfare must take precedence, and in any proceedings it is the court's paramount consideration when making any decision in relation to the child's care and upbringing.[26] This welfare test was not new to the Children Act and first appeared in s.1 of the Guardianship of Infants Act 1925, which stated that:

> Where any proceedings before any court...the custody or upbringing of an infant...[is] in question, the court, in deciding that question, shall regard the welfare of the infant as the first and paramount consideration.

Despite the passage of years, it is good to note that the thinking and language remain the same.

Therefore, before making its final decision, the court will also take into account other factors as set out in the Welfare Checklist,[27] and if there is a conflict between these considerations, then the child's welfare will overrule any other principle.[28]

If there are adoption proceedings, then this principle is extended under s.1(2) of the Adoption and Children Act 2002, which requires the court and adoption agencies to consider the child's welfare throughout their life.

26   S.1(1) Children Act 1989
27   S.1(3) Children Act 1989
28   S.1(1) Children Act 1989

The least interventionist approach

The local authority and the courts should operate on the least interventionist approach. This principle is based on the belief that children are generally best looked after within their own home and by their family, with least recourse to legal proceedings. For this reason, as highlighted earlier, the local authority's first duty is to provide support and services to maintain the child within the family or the wider family network, whilst at the same time ensuring that the child's welfare is protected.

This principle was firmly established in the Children Act 1989 with the No Order Principle, and further developed in the Children Act 2004 and the then Government's Every Child Matters agenda, which emphasised the need for early intervention in the lives of vulnerable children. This was to be achieved by identifying and providing effective support to parents to prevent the child's needs from escalating and thereby the child being at risk of poor outcomes.

If intervention is required that results in the removal of a child from their family, the local authority must firstly attempt all steps to return the child to their family as early as possible unless it is not reasonable to do so and is against the child's interests (HM Government, 2015, p 13 para 1.5). If it is not possible to return the child to their birth parents, the local authority must make every effort to consider placement within the extended family or persons connected to the family.

The No Order Principle

In court, the principle of the least interventionist approach is applied by having regard to the "No Order Principle", as set out in s.1(5) of the Children Act:

> *Where a court is considering whether or not to make one or more orders under this Act with respect to a child, it shall not make the order or any of the orders unless it considers that doing so would be better for the child than making no order at all.*

This means that the court will only make an order if it is satisfied that doing so is better for the child than making no order. If an order is necessary, the court will make the least interventionist or lesser order that meets the child's welfare, with the court having available to it the full range of orders within the Children Act.

The No Order Principle applies in both private and public law proceedings; for example, if the parents on their separation have made their own arrangements in relation to where the children are to live and when the children are to have contact with the non-resident parent. There will then be no need to make a child arrangements order, unless deemed necessary to give security to the arrangements.

The No Delay Principle

The court, when dealing with children's proceedings, will have regard to the "No Delay Principle". This means that delay in determining a question with respect to the upbringing of a child is considered likely to prejudice their welfare. Therefore, delay will not be acceptable to the court unless it is justifiable. This is strictly applied by the courts in care proceedings where a statutory time limit of 26 weeks was introduced by the Children and Families Act 2014.

Delay and drift in planning for a child, without justification, should always be avoided, even if there are no court proceedings. Delayed decisions in respect of intervention can result in children experiencing the cumulative jeopardy of lengthy exposure to abuse and neglect; disruption of attachments with temporary carers; unstable placements at home or in care; and children experiencing prolonged uncertainty about their future (Brown and Ward, 2012, p 72). Professor Eileen Munro recognised that drift and delay in making forthcoming plans for children have serious adverse effects on their development (2010, p 18, para 1.31). Even what may be considered as a short period of delay by adults can be perceived as an enormous period of time in a child's life. This was recognised by District Judge Crichton, who stated that: 'Two months of delay in making decisions in the best interest of a child or young person equates to one per cent of childhood that cannot be restored'.[29]

29   Judge Crichton (1 July 2010), Family Drug and Alcohol Court, London, *Munro Review of Child Protection Final Report*, May 2011

Principle of partnership

Although not explicitly referenced in the Children Act 1989, there is an expectation for children's services professionals to work in partnership with parents and carers in order to develop positive and open relationships.

What this means in practice is that, if the child is subject to an interim care order or a care order, the local authority shares parental responsibility with the parent/s who have parental responsibility. As they share this, the local authority must consult with those parents to seek their representations before making a decision in respect of the child. If there is conflict and the local authority is not in agreement with those who have parental responsibility, then the local authority should clearly communicate the reasons for its decision and why it is considered to be in the child's best interests.

When a child is subject to a care order, the local authority has the power to determine the extent to which a person with parental responsibility can exercise it (s.33(3)(b) Children Act 1989).

It is important to note that partnership with parents does not remove the local authority's overriding duty to safeguard and promote the child's welfare.

3.4 Interplay between the Children Act 1989 and human rights obligations

There is a great interplay between the Children Act 1989 and the International Conventions. The Human Rights Act 1998 protects individual rights as set out in the ECHR, and the UNCRC sets out the minimum standards of treatment towards children.

The interconnection between the Children Act 1989 and human rights issues is often raised in court proceedings. It was demonstrated in the leading Supreme Court case of *Re B (A Child)*,[30] which highlighted the relationship between the need to consider the child's welfare in accordance with the Children Act 1989 and the parties' Article 8 rights. This case concerned a child, A, aged three. In the care

---

30 *Re B (A Child) (Care Order)* [2013] UKSC 33

proceedings, the care plan for A presented to the court was adoption. The Judge clarified that a care plan for adoption should only be considered if there were no other realistic options.

The local authority must fully explore all available options for the child to remain in the family or friends network, even with support. This would enable the child to be raised within the family or wider family whilst protecting the child's Article 8 rights and equally ensuring that their welfare was protected. By granting the care order in respect of A, the Judge was interfering with the child's and parents' family life. Therefore, it is important that all realistic options have been fully explored and ruled out, and the adoption plan must be of "last resort".[31]

3.5   The Equality Act 2010

The Equality Act 2010 replaced previous anti-discrimination legislation, recognising the nine categories of protected characteristics: age, disability, gender assignment, marriage and civil partnership, pregnancy and maternity, race, religion or belief, sex, and sexual orientation. It places a statutory responsibility on local authorities to not only eliminate discrimination but also to promote equality and foster good relations. Social workers will already be familiar with anti-discriminatory practice from their academic studies. Social care professionals must have due regard to their statutory duty when working with children and families. They must ensure that no child or family is treated less favourably than others and that the child and the family are supported to fairly access available services and support, if a need is identified.

3.6   Statutory guidance

In addition to legislation, local authorities must also adhere to statutory guidance; a good example is *Working Together to Safeguard Children* (HM Government, 2018) (see below). Professionals must follow this unless there are sound local reasons to depart from it. Statutory guidance is often issued to support the understanding of new legislation.

31   *Re B (A Child) (Care Order)* [2013] UKSC 33, para 77

The legal status of statutory guidance is unusual, in that it is produced by the executive and not the legislator. If it is issued under s.7 of the Local Authority Social Services Act 1970, the guidance has the equivalent status as if it had been passed by Parliament:

Local authorities shall, in the exercise of their social services functions, including the exercise of any discretion conferred by any relevant enactment, act under the general guidance of the Secretary of State.

One of the core documents for multi-agency professionals is *Working Together to Safeguard Children* (HM Government, 2018). This is statutory guidance issued by the Government to support inter-agency working. It sets out a single set of rules and a clear national framework of guidance, placing a shared responsibility, and the need for effective joint working between agencies and professionals, in order to safeguard and promote children's welfare in accordance with primary legislation, in particular the Children Acts of 1989 and 2004. It is an extremely useful document and often an important starting point to understand how agencies such as police, local authorities, education and health services should work together for the protection of children. When there are substantial changes in the law, the guidance will be revised to reflect this. The latest edition of *Working Together* was issued in July 2018, replacing the 2015 edition, reflecting changes brought about by the Children and Social Work Act 2017.

Therefore, any guidance issued under s.7 of the Local Authority Social Services Act 1970 has the force of law as if it has been passed by Parliament, requiring local authorities to comply with the guidance unless there are justifiable reasons to depart from it. If the statutory guidance is not followed without sound justification, then children's services may be open to challenge by way of complaint or even possibly legal action by way of Judicial Review proceedings.

Equally, if a local authority acts outside of its statutory powers, such action can also be challenged through the complaints process or with the commencement of Judicial Review proceedings. These are legal proceedings requiring a High Court Judge to examine whether the local authority's actions are *"ultra vires"*, that is, whether the local authority has acted beyond its powers, unlawfully, or whether it has exercised its powers unreasonably. If such action is found, then the local authority will be directed by the court to review or rectify the process, for instance, by undertaking a fresh assessment.

3.7   Case law

Implementation of the Children Act 1989 came into force on 1 October 1991. How does this piece of legislation stay relevant in today's society? There are two ways in which this is achieved: firstly, from amendments being incorporated into the Children Act by later legislation such as the Adoption and Children Act 2002, the Children and Families Act 2014, and, more recently, the Children and Social Work Act 2017; and secondly, through case law, with the interpretation of the law by senior Judges when cases are before them.

Statutes passed by Parliament need to be drafted in broad language to cover a wide range of circumstances. When a case comes before a Judge, reliance on a particular section due to the way it has been drafted may appear vague or not applicable. The Judge's role is not to change the law laid down by Parliament; rather, through the judicial process, they assist with the interpretation of the law. If this judgement is made by a higher court, the judgement in the case is referred to as case law, which will then be influential on the lower courts. So case law issued from the Court of Appeal or the Supreme Court will create a binding precedent and influential guidance for the lower courts to follow. This process assists with developing consistency in the law's meaning and its application across all the courts. It also assists with the law's application to today's society and families. For the legislation to be relevant, it cannot remain static and has to be dynamic, adapting to society's changing needs. An illustration of this point can be highlighted in the interpretation of s.8 of the Children Act 1989, which details the provisions of child arrangements orders and other orders with respect to children in private law proceedings. (Child arrangements orders were introduced by the Children and Families Act 2014 and replaced the previous residence and contact orders.)

Child arrangements order means an order regulating arrangements relating to any of the following—

(a) with whom a child is to live, spend time or otherwise have contact, and

(b) when a child is to live, spend time or otherwise have contact with any person

(s.8(1) Children Act 1989)

When the Children Act 1989 was being drafted, it was based on the general understanding that, on the separation of a couple, the child or children would be in the care of one parent, with contact arrangements made for the other non-resident parent. If this could not be agreed, the court could grant a residence order to the resident parent/carer with whom the child/children were to reside and a contact order to the non-resident parent/carer.

In today's society, families are very different from how they were presented in the late 1980s. Today, it can be regarded as perfectly acceptable for parents to have children and choose not to live together, but want to undertake the long-term care of the children on a shared or joint basis. Case law has enabled recognition of these new forms of family arrangements and has now firmly established that joint and/or shared child arrangments orders can be made where they are manageable and suitable to meet the child's needs.

Case study 3: The family shares the responsibility

I qualified as a solicitor in 1995 and commenced my career as a local authority solicitor in 1997, as what were then known as local authority social services solicitors. One of the first care proceedings I undertook was a case my manager described as straightforward, based on the case facts. However, in my experience I have come to accept that there is no such concept as an "easy" or "straightforward" case, as was clearly demonstrated in the following case.

The so-called straightforward facts of the case were that a mother had given birth to a baby, who was suffering from drug withdrawal symptoms. Once the baby was ready for discharge, the baby was taken into voluntary care with the mother's consent, she being the only person with parental responsibility.[32] Both parents were long-term drug users; their addiction was funded by the mother

32 Under S.20 Children Act 1989.

who was described as working as an "active prostitute". (To this day, I do not know what a "inactive prostitute" means, but in any event I understood the nature of the concerns.) Upon the baby's birth, the local authority commenced care proceedings immediately thereafter. I came to know that this baby was in fact the mother's sixth child. What I found interesting was that none of her previous five children had been taken into care by any other local authority where the parents had previously lived.

On further investigation by the local authority, it was discovered that the older five children were being cared for by extended family members as part of a private family arrangement that had not required any input from children's services or legal orders. The family had formulated their unique long-term care plan for each of these five children. With each birth, the parents had handed the child over to the maternal grandmother who took care of the baby at her home until the child was ready to commence pre-school education. Thereafter, the child's care and residence transferred to the maternal aunt's care, where the child would remain until they were ready to transfer to secondary school. From then on, the child's care and residence transferred back to the maternal grandmother's care. This enabled the older children to assist the grandmother in caring for the younger pre-school children in the maternal grandmother's home.

Every Sunday, all the children, including the maternal aunt's own birth children, would get together for a family Sunday lunch at the maternal grandmother's home. The parents were also invited but knew that they could only attend if they were not under the influence of drugs or alcohol. All the children understood their position in the family, were aware of their situation, and welcomed the contact that they had with their parents as and when this happened. The children were thriving, meeting their developmental milestones in the maternal grandmother's and maternal aunt's joint care.

So, when considering a care plan for this new baby, it was clear that this family had a working care plan; it was tried and tested, and it would be equally suitable for this baby. The family members and the parents fully supported the baby being placed with the siblings in the same way. Also, placing the child within the wider family would mean that both the family's and the child's Article 8 rights were being respected.

Special guardianship orders had not yet been legally introduced at this time and so, at the final hearing, the local authority recommended a joint residence order (which would now be deemed to be a child arrangements order) so that both the maternal grandmother and aunt could share parental responsibility with the parents. A joint order was the preferred option as it enabled the maternal grandmother and aunt to share joint care of the child at different stages of the child's development.

If the same case facts were presented today, a special guardianship order to both the maternal grandmother and aunt could also have been an option. The special guardianship order does not specify where the child is to live and so the child could change residence as and when the carers deemed this necessary. The special guardianship order would only have been a preferred option if the maternal grandmother and aunt required the need to exercise parental responsibility to the exclusion of the parents. This was not required in this case as the parents were in complete agreement and were not attempting to exercise their parental responsibility over and above the maternal aunt or grandmother. Therefore, in accordance with the least interventionist approach, a child arrangements order could still be considered a suitable order.

2

The child's voice v parental rights

1   Ascertaining the child's wishes and feelings

It is widely acknowledged that, to keep children safe, professionals must listen to them and give serious consideration to what they say. When a child is listened to, this can lead to a trusting relationship with their social worker. Being listened to gives them the opportunity to ask questions, to be consulted on decisions, and can enable them to feel they are being kept informed, all very important for both child and worker to develop a trusting and meaningful relationship.

The importance of listening to children was highlighted in the report, *People Like Us*, by Sir William Utting (1997), commissioned in the wake of allegations of abuse of children living in care homes and foster care in Wales. The report acknowledged the need to involve children and young people in developing policy, for their views to be taken into account, and the need to improve professionals' communication skills (p 8).

Despite an awareness of the significance of listening to children, there has been persistent criticism in past Inquiries and Serious Case Reviews into child deaths that professionals fail to speak or listen to the children involved and that children are often overlooked. The key obstacles in professionals' communication with children were identified by Professor Eileen Munro: that the social worker may lack the skills, or not have sufficient time due to the pressures of frontline practice (2011). Another hindrance is that children's views can be lost in the face of adults' complex needs and vulnerabilities (Fauth *et al*, 2010).

It is important for professionals to understand that listening to children should be undertaken in an active, not a passive, way. This was identified by the Care Inquiry

(2013), that was set up to look at how best to provide stable and permanent homes for vulnerable children who cannot live with their parents. One of its many recommendations was that professionals and carers must value children's "active contributions". Article 12 of the UNCRC reiterates the principle of active participation by the child:

States Parties shall assure to the child who is capable of forming his or her own views the right to express those views freely in all matters affecting the child, the views of the child being given due weight in accordance with the age and maturity of the child.

This means that all children and young people have a right to active participation and an opportunity to express and have their views taken into account in all matters that affect them; this includes children with disabilities (Article 23).

The concept of listening to and ascertaining the child's wishes and feelings has been fully enshrined throughout the Children Act 1989. Article 12 of the UNCRC has been incorporated into s.22(4) of the Children Act 1989, which states that a local authority:

Before making any decision with respect to a child who the local authority is proposing to or is looking after shall, as far as is reasonably practicable, ascertain the wishes and feelings of:

(a) the child;

(b) his parents;

(c) any person who is not a parent of his but who has parental responsibility for him; and

(d) any other person whose wishes and feelings the authority consider to be relevant.

regarding the matter that is to be decided.

The significance of s.1(3) of the Children Act 1989 has already been discussed, this sets out the Welfare Checklist, the criteria that the court has to consider before it makes a decision in any family proceedings. As stated, the first criterion of the Welfare Checklist is that the court must consider the ascertainable wishes and feelings of the child concerned, in light of their age and understanding. In court, the child's views will be reported to the court by the child's social worker and a Children's Guardian (appointed by the court from CAFCASS) in public law proceedings, and by a Family Court Adviser (appointed from CAFCASS) in private law proceedings.

In practice, in order for professionals to ascertain the wishes and feelings of children, this is undertaken in two parts: firstly, the social worker or CAFCASS officer must ascertain the child's wishes and feelings. If the child is verbal, and if considered appropriate, this can be done by speaking to the child. If this is not possible, either because the child is non-verbal or if otherwise not considered appropriate, then professionals will use various tools or resources and engage in direct work with the child to assess their wishes and feelings. Secondly, the professionals must consider whether it is possible to act upon these wishes and feelings in light of the child's age, understanding and their welfare.

Section 22(5) of the Children Act 1989 requires that the local authority, when making any decision, should give due consideration to these wishes and feelings, having regard to the child's understanding, religious persuasion, racial origin, and cultural and linguistic background.

The Children Act 2004 further protects the key principle of listening and having due regard to the child's views by amending s.17, s.20 and s.47 of the Children Act 1989, to include the need to, as far as possible, ascertain the child's wishes and feelings in relation to provision of services or before making a decision.

The legislation could not be clearer, requiring professionals to engage with the child or young person, ensuring that their participation and voice are heard in decision making. For this to be effective, the child/young person will need to be kept fully informed. Professionals will use different skills, tools or resources, depending on the child's age and understanding, to assist them in this process. This practice is particularly important where there are no court proceedings, as prior to commencement of any care proceedings, the child is not independently represented. Therefore, their voice will only be heard via the child's social worker who, after ascertaining the child's wishes and feelings, should clearly record this in the assessment document and the case notes held in the child's file.

The children looked after (CLA) review is a key meeting where children will have a further opportunity for their views to be heard and considered. Section 22(4) is repeated at s.26(2)(d) of the Children Act 1989, which also requires that the child's views be sought at any CLA reviews.[33]

Children's views must be actively pursued by the social worker prior to the CLA review and by the Independent Reviewing Officer (IRO) at the review. Children are invited and actively encouraged to attend their review, if they wish to do so. However, for this to be an effective process, children need to be informed and prepared so that they can actively participate with meaning and purpose. This process should not be considered a "tick-box" exercise, as can be demonstrated by a young man speaking of his experience of attending his review:

> I was never asked about how I felt or what I wanted to happen. Asking me 10 minutes before the meeting is not the same.

(Munro, 2011)

The second stage of this process is for the professional to consider whether they can act on the child's wishes and feelings. If they cannot, then the reason needs to be explained to the child, in a way and using language that the child will understand. The child's social worker should also record the reason how (if possible) it was explained to the child and the child's reaction in the child's file so that there is a clear record that will be available to the child, should they wish to access their file in the future.

2 Parental rights and responsibilities

The evolution of children's rights and erosion of parental rights have already been discussed in Chapter 1, along with how the Children Act 1989 recognised the shift from parental rights to parental responsibility.

---

33 S.26(d)(i) Children Act 1989

2.1 Parenthood

Before exploring who has parental responsibility, it is important to identify who parents are. A child, when born, can only have two legal parents; however, the courts have recognised three different types of parents.

In the case of *Re G*,[34] the court considered the concept of family and recognised three ways in which a person can become a parent, differentiating between a natural and a legal parent.

1. Biological/genetic parenthood provides the gametes, that is, the sex cells that unite to produce the child. The male gametes are the sperm, and the female gametes are the eggs. Knowledge of a child's origins and lineage is important in helping the child to find a sense of self as they grow up.[35]

2. Gestational parenthood conceives and bears the child. The mother who bears the child is legally the child's mother even if the gametes (eggs) do not belong to her. The status of this parent recognises a special relationship between the gestational mother, who carries the foetus, and the child.[36]

3. Social and psychological parenthood. Here, the parent may not be genetically or legally connected to the child, but develops a relationship with them by providing for their needs at both the basic level of feeding, nurturing, comforting and loving, followed by the more sophisticated level of guiding, socialising, educating and protecting.[37] The concept of "psychological parenthood" was developed in 1973 and defined as:

One who, on a continuous, day-to-day basis, through interaction, companionship, interplay, and mutuality, fulfils the child's psychological needs for a parent, as well as the child's physical needs.

(Solnit *et al*, 1973)

---

34 *Re G* [2006] UKHL 43
35 *Re G* [2006] UKHL 43, para 33
36 *Re G* [2006] UKHL 43, para 34
37 *Re G* [2006] UKHL 43, para 35

A psychological parent can be a biological parent, adopter, agency foster carer, private foster carer, kinship carer/special guardian, or connected person.

In many cases, the natural/birth mother may combine all three types of parents: she will be the genetic, gestational and psychological parent. The natural/ birth father may be a combination of the genetic and psychological parent. It is important to understand the differing status of parenthood, particularly for those children who may have experienced a variety of parentage.

2.2   Definition of parental responsibility

The Children Act 1989 defines parental responsibility at s.3(1) as:

> *...all the rights, duties, powers, responsibilities and authority which by law a parent of a child has in relation to the child and his property.*

The Act recognises that parents have a collection of duties, rights and authority in respect of their child's life, enabling the parents to make day-to-day decisions. These rights grouped together are known as parental responsibility:

> *The Children Act does not place the primary responsibility of bringing up children upon judges, magistrates, CAFCASS officers or courts; the responsibility is placed upon the child's parents. Whether or not a parent has parental responsibility is not simply a matter that achieves the ticking of a box on a form. It is a significant matter of status as between parent and child and, just as important, as between each of the parents.*

(MacFarlane LJ, *Re W (Children)*)[38]

There is no precise list of matters that a parent with parental responsibility has the right to do in respect of the child. Parental responsibility permits the person who has it to make important decisions in respect of the child, such as which school the child is to attend, overseas travel, consent for medical treatment, the child's religion, or consent to the child's adoption.

The principle of parental responsibility is flexible, in that:

38   *Re W (Children)* [2012] EWCA 999

- There are no limits to how many people can have parental responsibility for a child. Therefore, more than one person may have parental responsibility at the same time.[39]

- Parental responsibility does not cease merely because some other person subsequently acquires it; for example, if it is acquired by a local authority on the granting of an interim care order or care order, or if an individual acquires parental responsibility by means of a court order, such as a child arrangements order or special guardianship order.[40] With the exception of an adoption order, the acquisition of parental responsibility does not extinguish the parent's parental responsibility, although it may affect their right to exercise it.

- A person with parental responsibility may not surrender or transfer any part of it to another. However, they can arrange for some or all of it to be met by one or more persons acting on their behalf. Thus, parental responsibility may be delegated but not transferred, and the person who delegates it remains liable for meeting their responsibility.[41] An example where this may happen is in private fostering arrangements, where a parent requests a person who is not a close relative to care for their child who is aged 16 or under (or under 18, if disabled) for 28 days or more.[42] A close relative is defined as someone who is not a grandparent, brother, sister, uncle or aunt, whether by blood (full or half), marriage, civil partnership or a step-parent.[43]

- Parental responsibility alone does not make the person who has it a parent or relative of the child in legal terms, if they are not already one. It does not provide any rights of inheritance, nor does it place upon the person with parental responsibility a statutory duty to financially maintain the child.[44]

Parental responsibility is not an absolute and immovable right, as the need to exercise it lessens as the child acquires maturity. Therefore, those with parental

39 S.2(5) Children Act 1989
40 S.2(6) Children Act 1989
41 S.2(11) Children Act 1989
42 S.66 Children Act 1989
43 S.105 Children Act 1989
44 S.3(4) Children Act 1989

responsibility have the right to exercise it; however, this legal right decreases as the child matures. In practice, this means that the power to exercise parental responsibility also reduces simultaneously as the child matures, increasing the child's right to be heard and ability to make decisions for themselves, and the parents' rights to exercise parental responsibility becoming more of providing guidance. For example, if a young person is 16 and requests local authority accommodation, then even if the parent with parental responsibility objects, the local authority can provide accommodation for the child, if it is assessed as necessary to do so. This ability for a child to make decisions as they mature, and for the decision to be acted upon even if the parent opposes it, was firmly established in the case of *Gillick v West Norfolk and Wisbech Area Health Authority*.[45] In this case, Mrs Gillick, a mother of five daughters under the age of 16, sought a declaration that it would be unlawful for a doctor to prescribe contraceptives to girls under 16 without the parents' knowledge or consent. It was held that 'parental authority ceases in respect of any aspect of a child's upbringing about which the child himself is sufficiently mature to make decisions for himself'. It is therefore a decreasing right, as identified in the earlier *Hewer v Byrant*, by Lord Denning, who clarified parental responsibility as:

> *The legal right of a parent, ends at the eighteenth birthday, and even up till then, it is a dwindling right which the court will hesitate to enforce against the wishes of the child, the older he is. It starts with a right of control and ends with little more than advice.*[46]

This case is also important as it illustrates Lord Denning's forward thinking on the need for the law to be dynamic, and that the law is adaptable to accommodate changing times. He rejected the notion of the absolute authority of parents over children, as exemplified by the Victorian parent, taking the view that common law 'can and should keep pace with the times'.[47] The Judges in the Gillick case relied heavily on what Lord Denning said in the earlier case, recognising that the parents did not have absolute control over their children. In the Gillick case, Lord Scarman stated that:

45 *Gillick v West Norfolk & Wisbech Area Health Authority* [1986] AC 112
46 *Hewer v Bryant* [1970] 1 QB 357, para 369
47 *Hewer v Bryant* [1970] 1 QB 357, para 369

Parental rights do clearly exist, and they do not wholly disappear until the age of majority...but the common law has never treated such rights as sovereign or beyond review and control...the principle of the law...is that parental rights are derived from parental duty and exist only so long as they are needed for the protection of the person or property of the child.[48]

Therefore, as recognised by Lord Scarman above, parental rights are not absolute and must be exercised in accordance with the welfare principle, and can be challenged, and even overridden, if necessary.

The Gillick case firmly recognised that the rights existed for the benefit of the child and not just the parent, that there are legal limits to parental rights, and that these are dwindling rights, ending when the child reaches 18. Further, in the event of a conflict between the parent's views and competent child's views, then subject to the child's welfare it is the child's views that should be given priority.

What these cases also established is that the capacity of a child to be involved in making decisions is not dependent on their age, but rather their level of maturity and understanding.

Equally, as the child's age increases, the law recognises their right and ability to make decisions for themselves. For example, if a child is 16 or over, the Family Law Reform Act 1969 provides that the child may consent to their own medical treatment, even if this is against their parents' wishes. However, the decision can be overridden by the courts, based on the paramountcy principle.

2.3   Who has parental responsibility?

Parental responsibility gives automatic legal rights over a child. The Family Justice Review (set up in 2010 to consider reforms for the family justice system) found a lack of understanding about parental responsibility, including the mistaken belief that the balance of parental responsibility shifts following separation of the parents, with one parent assuming full responsibility for their child (Family Justice Final Report, November 2011, para 106). It is therefore important to be clear from the outset as to who has parental responsibility for the child and how it has been

48 Lord Scarman, *Gillick v West Norfolk and Wisbech Area Health Authority* [1986] AC 112

acquired. The legal rules on this are set out in s.2 of the Children Act 1989 and are dependent on the person's legal relationship to the child.

Birth mother

Birth mother means the woman who gave birth to the child; she has automatic parental responsibility on the birth of the child, irrespective of whether she is married to the father.[49] The birth mother's parental responsibility can only be removed if the child is adopted or, at present in surrogacy arrangements, with the making of a parental order (s.54 Human Fertilisation and Embryology Act 2008).

Fathers who are married/in a civil partnership

If the father is married to or in a civil partnership with the mother, he will also have parental responsibility automatically on the birth of the child. This also applies if he marries or enters into a civil partnership with the mother after the birth of the child, thereby legitimising the child.

Once this right is acquired by the married father, it is unaffected by the physical separation of parents or legal dissolution of the marriage, thereby acknowledging that even if the parents' relationship ends, this does not impact on the ongoing legal responsibility a parent has towards their child.

If the parents are married, then either parent can register the child's birth and both the husband's and wife's details will be entered on the child's birth certificate.

Fathers who are not married/in a civil partnership

If the father is registered jointly with the mother on the child's birth certificate after 1 December 2003,[50] then the father will have automatic parental responsibility. If the father's name is registered prior to this date, it does not automatically give the unmarried/not civilliy partnered father parental responsibility.

49 s.2(1) and s2(2) Children Act 1989

50 S.4(1)(a) Children Act 1989 – change brought about further to enactment of the Adoption and Children Act 2002.

In order to register the unmarried/not civilly partnered father on the child's birth certificate, the father has to be present at the time of registration, or if not present the unmarried father can sign a statutory declaration agreeing for his name to be placed on the certificate in his absence.

A court can also make an order for a father to be named on a child's birth certificate.

If the unmarried/not civilly partnered father is not registered at the time of registration of the child's birth certificate, then he can acquire parental responsibility by:

- marrying the mother after the birth of the child; or by

- entering into a parental responsibility agreement with the mother's consent.[51] The agreement is a prescribed form obtained from the court. Once signed by both parents, the agreement needs to be registered with the court. Once registered, it has the same effect as if the father had been granted a parental responsibility order.

It should be noted that although parents can enter into the agreement for the father to acquire parental responsibility, they cannot enter into an agreement to terminate the father's parental responsibility. It will end only when the child attains the age of 18 or if the agreement is terminated by a court order.

If the mother does not agree to enter into a parental responsibility agreement, then the unmarried/not civilly partnered father can apply for a parental responsibility order.[52] The court will require evidence that the unmarried/not civilly partnered father is the child's biological father; if this is disputed by the mother, the court can direct DNA testing.[53]

- The court is likely to grant a parental responsibility order if the father can demonstrate the following:

    - commitment, that is, the father's degree of commitment to the child;

51 S.4(1)(b) Children Act 1989
52 S.4(1)(c) Children Act 1989
53 *Re F (A Minor) (Blood Tests)* [1993] 1 FLR 598

- attachment or current relationship between the father and child; and

- motivation and intention, that is, the father's reason for making the application.[54]

There is no presumption of the granting of parental responsibility; however, it would be an exceptional case where it was not awarded.

With any Children Act application, the court will also have regard to the welfare principle as set out in s.1(1) of the Children Act 1989. This was illustrated in the case of *Re B (Role of Biological Father)*.[55] The child was conceived as a result of the father donating his sperm to a same-sex female couple. The relations were further complicated in that the birth father was also the non-birth mother's brother. The birth father agreed that the child would be raised by the same-sex couple but also wanted parental responsibility. He applied for a parental responsibility order and successfully showed commitment, attachment and motivation. However, it was considered by the Judge not to be appropriate to grant the father a parental responsibility order and not in the child's best interests as it would undermine the same-sex couple's parenting of the child.

In the case of *PM v MB & Anor*,[56] the Judge clarified that the granting of parental responsibility was not to be "automatically conferred" if the father posed a risk to a child or if the father's reasons for applying were "demonstrably wrong", and likely misuse of parental responsibility could lead to it being refused.

A court would not refuse consideration to grant a parental responsibility order simply because:

- The father could not show a likelihood of being able to exercise parental responsibility but could show commitment.

- The mother is unwilling and even hostile to the father's involvement in the child's life, perhaps because the mother has moved on in her life or has a new relationship and wants the child to develop a relationship with her

---

54 *Re H (Minors) (Local Authority: Parental Rights)* (No 3) [1991] 2 WLR 763
55 *Re B (Role of Biological Father)* [2008] 1 FLR 1015
56 *PM v MB & Anor* [2013] EWCA Civ 969

new partner, fearing that involvement by the birth father will interfere in this. In such cases, the court is concerned only with the child's welfare in accordance with s.1(1) of the Children Act 1989. However, the court has demonstrated creativity and considered ways in which the father could exercise parental responsibility, without resulting in him facing conflict with the mother. In the cases *Re G (A Minor) (Parental Responsibility Order)*[57] and *B v A and Others (Parental Responsibility)*,[58] the court granted the father a parental responsibility order; however, it restricted his exercise of parental responsibility in that he was not to contact the child's health care professionals or school without the consent of the mother or her female partner, who both shared a residence order (which would now be deemed to be a child arrangements order).

– A parental responsibility order may not be granted if there are concerns that the father may abuse his parental responsibility.[59]

– If the father is granted a child arrangements order and the court has directed that the child is to reside with the father,[60] the court must also make a parental responsibility order in respect of the father. If the child arrangements order provides for the father to have contact with the child but not to live with him, the court must consider whether it would be appropriate to also make a parental responsibility order. The parental responsibility order can only be brought to an end by further order of the court; however, the court may not terminate a father's parental responsibility while a child arrangements order is in place providing that the child should live with him.

The two orders are separate, as illustrated by *Re C and V (Contact and Parental Responsibility)*,[61] which made it very clear that where there is an application for a parental responsibility order alongside what was then a contact order (now a

---

57 *Re G (A Minor) (Parental Responsibility Order)* [1994] 1 FLR 504

58 *B v A and Others (Parental Responsibility)* [2006] EWHC 2 (Fam)

59 *Re P (Parental Responsibility)* [1998] 2 FLR 96

60 S.12(1) Children Act 1989

61 *Re C and V (Contact and Parental Responsibility)* [1998] 1 FLR 392

child arrangements order), the court should not refuse a parental responsibility application simply because it had decided not to grant contact.

Parental responsibility agreements and parental responsibility orders remain in effect until the child is 18, unless revoked by the court.

Absent fathers

All attempts should be made to locate absent fathers, whether they have parental responsibility or not when children's services become involved in their child's life. Just because they are absent, they should not be forgotten. It was reported in the serious case review relating to Baby P (Peter Connelly) that the birth father was not notified when his two children (who were living in the same household as Baby P) were placed on the child protection register. The father only became aware when the mother, Tracey Connelly, brought it to his attention (Haringey Local Safeguarding Children Board, 2009, p 8). It is important for social workers to inform the other parent and anyone else who has parental responsibility, such as a special guardian, of children's services' involvement.

Step-parents

Section 4A of the Children Act 1989 (which took effect from 30 December 2005) enables step-parents (married or civil partner to the birth parent) to acquire parental responsibility by:

- entering into a parental responsibility agreement with their spouse in relation to the spouse's child with the consent of anyone else who has parental responsibility for the child; or

- seeking a parental responsibility order.

Same-sex couples

a. Two female parents

In law, a child can only have two parents; that is, the mother and her partner, or the mother and father.

The Marriage (Same-Sex Couples) Act 2013 provides that a same-sex marriage has no relevance as to who a child's parents are. This means that a female spouse is not automatically considered the other parent.

The father is to be considered as the legal second parent if the mother is not in a civil partnership or married and she and her same-sex partner did not comply with the requirements of the Human Fertility and Embryology Act 2008.

b. Civil partners/married couple

If the female same-sex couple are in a civil partnership or married and their child was conceived through artificial insemination subject to the provisions of the Human Fertilisation and Embryology Act after 6 April 2009,[62] the legal parents are the gestational mother and the civil partner or wife. Once the child is born, both their names can be entered on the birth certificate and both will then automatically have parental responsibility.[63] If the child was conceived through sexual intercourse with the father, then the father will be considered the legal second parent; however, he will not acquire parental responsibility automatically.

If the child was conceived prior to 6 April 2009, the second female spouse or civil partner can acquire parental responsibility by entering with the birth mother into a parental responsibility agreement or applying for a parental responsibility or child arrangements order.[64]

c. Non-civil partners/unmarried couple

If the same-sex female couple are not married or in a civil partnership, and the child was not conceived at a licensed fertility clinic, the partner will not automatically have any parental responsibility but can acquire it if they are granted a child arrangements or parental responsibility order. They can also enter into a parental responsibility agreement or jointly register the child's birth.

62 Human Fertilsation and Embryology Act 2008
63 S.4Z(A)(1)(a) Children Act 1989
64 S.4Z(A)(1)(b) & (c) Children Act 1989

d. Two male parents

Two male parents can acquire parental responsibility by adopting the child or through surrogacy, on the granting of a parental order.

A male partner of a birth (biological) father who has been granted a parental order following a surrogacy arrangement can acquire parental responsibility either by entering into a parental responsibility agreement or by being granted a parental responsibility order.

Surrogacy

Surrogacy is where a woman agrees to carry a child on behalf of someone else, with the intention that she does not wish to parent the child and agrees to transfer the legal parenting rights to the commissioning parent/s. This way of becoming a parent is increasing in the UK. The current legislation is governed by the Surrogacy Arrangements Act 1985, and certain provisions of the Human Fertilisation and Embryology Act 2008 are also applicable.

At present, the law states that the intended parent/s who "commission" the surrogacy arrangement do not have parental responsibility for the child at the time of their birth. However, the biological father can be a legal parent and can register his name on the child's birth certificate, if the surrogate is not married. The commissioning parent/s can obtain a parental order to transfer the parental responsibility from the surrogate mother and/or the biological father to them. For the order to be granted, the child must be living with the commissioning parent/s, must be the biological child of one of the parents, and the application must be made within six months of the child's birth. The surrogate mother must agree to the making of a parental order and understand the consequences of it; namely that it transfers her parental responsibility to the commissioning parent/s.

I have already highlighted the need for the law to stay relevant, by adapting to the changing demands and attitudes in today's society. There has been recognition of the need for the law relating to surrogacy arrangements to be reformed to adjust and accommodate to its increasing demand. As a result, the Law Commission is currently reviewing the law following a public consultation.

The final report from the Law Commission with its recommendations for reform of the law and a draft bill are expected to be presented to Parliament in 2021.

Kinship carers

If the child is being cared for by a kinship or connected carer, and if they are granted a child arrangements order[65] or special guardianship order,[66] they will acquire parental responsibility for the child while the order remains in effect.

Non-parent carers

If a local authority is granted an emergency protection order (EPO),[67] interim care order (ICO)[68] or care order,[69] it will acquire parental responsibility for the duration of the order, and the exercise of it is limited in the case of an EPO and ICO. The local authority will share parental responsibility with the parents, as parents do not lose parental responsibility. For that reason, the local authority, when making any decision for a child subject to a care order, must always consult with those parents who have parental responsibility. It must also provide an opportunity for the parents to make representations, particularly if they disagree with the authority. However, once the parents have been consulted and their representations considered, the local authority has the right to make the final decision in relation to the child and has the power to determine the extent to which a parent or anyone else with parental responsibility can exercise it.[70] The local authority can decide not to permit those with whom it shares parental responsibility the ability to exercise aspects of their parental responsibility, if it is satisfied that this is necessary to safeguard and promote the child's welfare.[71]

---

65 S.8 Children Act 1989

66 S.14 Children Act 1989

67 S.44 Children Act 1989

68 S.38 Children Act 1989

69 S.31 Children Act 1989

70 S.33(3) Children Act 1989

71 S.33(4) Children Act 1989

Adoptive parents

When a child is placed with prospective adoptive parents under a placement order, they acquire parental responsibility for that child.[72] The parental responsibility is shared with the birth parents and the local authority; however, the local authority has the power to decide to what extent the birth parents and prospective adopters can exercise that parental responsibility.

On the making of an adoption order, the adoptive parents are granted parental responsibility for the child and it extinguishes the birth parents' and the local authority's parental responsibility, if the child was subject to a placement order.[73]

It should be noted that the granting of an adoption order to a step-parent, who is the partner (married or civil) of the birth parent, will not affect the parental responsibility of the birth parent with whom they are in a relationship.

A carer who has no parental responsibility

Any person caring for a child who does not have parental responsibility may do what is "reasonable in the circumstances" to safeguard or promote the child's welfare.[74] This can include, for example, a foster carer, teacher, or health staff.

Testamentary Guardian

A parent with parental responsibility may appoint a guardian either in their will or other written document. The guardian will have parental responsibility for the child upon the death of the parent, unless the child has another living parent with parental responsibility, in which case the guardian's appointment will not take effect whilst the other parent has parental responsibility.[75]

---

72 S.25(2) Adoption and Children Act 2002
73 S.46(2)(a) Adoption and Children Act 2002
74 S.3(5) Children Act 1989
75 S.5 Children Act 1989

2.4 Termination of parental responsibility

Parental responsibility can end in a number of ways:

- When the child reaches majority, at age 18.

- When the young person marries between the ages of 16–18 years.

- By court order, terminating the parental responsibility order.

- Where parental responsibility has been acquired with the granting of an order, such as a child arrangements order, special guardianship order, emergency protection order, interim care order or care order, then if the order is discharged (or in the case of an emergency protection order, lapses), then the acquired parental responsibility will end. For that reason, the Children Act 1989 specifies that where the court makes a child arrangements order for unmarried fathers, it must also make a parental responsibility order. This would mean that if the child arrangements order was no longer in force, the unmarried father's parental responsibility will still be retained as a result of the parental responsibility order.

- Adoption of the child will terminate the birth parents' parental responsibility permanently. The adoption order results in the parents' parental responsibility being extinguished and parental responsibility being granted to the adopters. The making of an adoption order severs any legal links between the child and their birth parents, and in law it is as if the child was born to the adopters.

- Parental responsibility can be terminated by the ending of a parental responsibility agreement through a court order.

- A person's parental responsibility terminates on their death. However, as previously discussed, a person with parental resonsibility may appoint a testamentary guardian who will acquire parental responsibility for the child if there is no one else living who has parental responsibility.

Termination of a person's parental responsibility by court order is a serious step, as recognised in the case *Re P (Terminating Parental Responsibility)*.[76] In that case,

---

76 *Re P (Terminating Parental Responsibility)* [1995] 1 FLR 1048

the Judge allowed an application to terminate parental responsibility (acquired by a parental responsibility agreement) in relation to a father who had been sent to prison for causing serious injuries to his child. The Judge held that the order was justified as the father had "forfeited" his parental responsibility and, in considering the merits of the application for parental responsibility in these circumstances, a court would not have granted the application.

The Judge emphasised the unusual and draconian nature of the decision to terminate the parental responsibility order and indicated that it should not be:

> ...a weapon in the hands of the dissatisfied mother of the non-marital child: it should be used by the court as an appropriate step in the regulation of the child's life where the circumstances really do warrant it and not otherwise.[77]

The Judge's approach in this earlier case was adopted in Re D (A Child).[78] This was an appeal of the earlier, lower court's decision to terminate the father's parental responsibility. The parties were never married and on the birth of D (2004), the father acquired parental responsibility by virtue of being named on D's birth certificate.[79] In 2009, the father pleaded guilty to sexual offences against the mother's two daughters from a previous relationship. He was sentenced to 48 months' imprisonment.

Immediately upon his release from prison, the applicant mother issued an application for the termination of his parental responsibility. The respondent father applied for a specific issue order, requiring the mother to supply annual reports as to the child's progress.

The Judge concluded that the factors in this case were D's emotional needs, the harm he had suffered, and the risk of future harm.[80] Following the earlier Re P, the Judge found that there was no element of the bundle of responsibilities that make up parental responsibility which this father could in present or foreeable circumstances exercise in a way that would be beneficial for D. The

---

77   Re P (Terminating Parental Responsibility) [1995] 1 FLR 1048
78   Re D (A Child) [2014] EWCA Civ 315, also cited as CW v SG [2013] EWHC 854 (Fam)
79   S.4(1) Children Act 1989
80   Re D (A Child) [2014] EWCA Civ 315, para 25

Judge concluded that D's emotional security would be imperilled were the father to continue to have any further involvement in his life. Equally, whilst the Judge acknowledged the Article 8 rights for D and his father to have a family life together, these were outweighed by D's overriding need as part of his Article 8 rights to security within his family.[81] The father's parental responsibility was terminated and his application for a specific issue order under s.8 of the Children Act 1989 rejected. This was upheld in the Court of Appeal, where the father's appeal was dismissed. The court emphasised that when considering the continuance of parental responsibility, this legal status is related to the child's welfare and that the paramountcy principle is overarching. It also reiterated that it is the child's welfare that creates a "presumption" as to the existence or continuance of parental responsibility, not the fact of the father's parenthood or parental rights.

2.5   Conflict in the exercise of parental responsibility

Where there is conflict between those who have parental responsibility, s.8 of the Children Act 1989 provides the court with the ability to make prohibited steps orders or specific issue orders.

Prohibited steps order

This is an order preventing or restraining a person with parental responsibility from taking any step in relation to a child that could be taken by a parent in meeting their parental responsibility, without consent of the court. It can be used, for example, in restraining a parent with parental responsibility from removing the child from the UK, preventing a change of school, or prohibiting them from contacting the child at home or school.

Specific issue order

This order is used where those with parental responsibility cannot agree on a specific matter. The court is requested to resolve the specific issue or dispute that has arisen in connection with an aspect of parental responsibility for the child by

81   *Re D (A Child)* [2014] EWCA Civ 315, para 58

giving directions. It can be used, for example, to resolve disputes about a child's surname, education, religious upbringing or medical treatment.

In the case of *Re S (Children) (Specific Issue Order: Religion: Circumcision)*,[82] the mother and father, who had two children, were separated. The mother applied for permission for her children to become practising members of the Islamic faith and for her son, K, to be circumcised. K was eight-and-a-half years old. The father, who followed the Jain religion, opposed the application; he wished the children to experience both the Islamic faith and Jainism. He felt that the children could decide which faith to follow when they were older and more mature. The father's concern was that if the children became practising Muslims, it would not allow them to take part in Jain religious events. The father also considered the circumcision to be a form of unacceptable mutilation.

The court recognised that the children were of mixed cultural heritage and knew life as both Muslims and Jains. The mother's application stemmed from her need to secure her religious marriage to a Muslim man and was not directly related to the children's needs. The court would not sanction this and recognised that if the children became fully practising Muslims, they would not be permitted to join in the Jain religious events. The court took the view that as K had been ambivalent about his religion, and as he was not old enough to understand the long-term implications that once circumcision was done it could not be undone, the court held that it was not in K's best interests for him to be circumcised, that he could decide to do this once he reached puberty when he was "Gillick competent".

The courts can face these types of applications in relation to urgent medical treatment for children where again parents do not agree. In the case of *Z v Y*,[83] the mother made an application for a specific issue order for her daughter A, who was seven years old, to undergo brain surgery to alleviate epileptic seizures. The mother wanted A to have the surgery, believing it was the best chance for A to become seizure free. The father opposed it as the success rate of the surgery was only 50 per cent. The Judge, having undertaken a thorough analysis of the

---

82 *Re S (Children) (Specific Issue Order: Religion: Circumcision)* [2004] EWHC 1282 (Fam); [2005] 1 FLR 236; [2004] Fam Law 869

83 *Z v Y* [2019] EWHC 2255 (Fam)

welfare checklist, the negatives and positives of the surgery and the paramountcy principle, ordered that the surgery should go ahead and made a specific issue order to that effect.

It should be noted that the court will not make a prohibited steps order or a specific issue order for a child who is in the care of the local authority.[84]

84 S.9(1) and s.9(2) Children Act 1989

3

Introduction to the Lesland case study

This case study, which is ongoing throughout the guide, explores the Lesland family and follows the children's journey through the different legal processes, and is included to assist readers in understanding the key legal stages.

It is important to note that this case study is not a template for every child's journey through the legal process, as each child will have their own unique journey dependent on the facts of their case.

Family composition

Name	Sex, and relationship status	Age and circumstances	Ethnicity
Rachel Gill	Female	Aged 10	Mixed ethnicity
Josh Gill	Male	Aged 8 Has learning difficulties and is diagnosed as autistic	Mixed ethnicity
Caroline Lesland	Female	Aged 1	White British
Mrs Mary Lesland	Mother	Aged 34	White British
Mr Kevin Lesland	Father of Caroline	Aged 48	White British

Mr Thomas Gill	Father of Rachel and Josh Gill	Current whereabouts unknown	Black African
Mrs Lesland, Senior (widow)	Paternal grandmother of Caroline	Aged 75	White British
Mr Andrew Price and Mrs Alice Price (deceased)	Maternal grandparents		White British
Kalisha Petal	Maternal aunt	Aged 36	White British
Peter Price	Maternal uncle	Aged 40	White British

The Lesland case: Part 1

Mrs Mary Lesland (mother) and Mr Kevin Lesland have been married for one year. They have been in a relationship for two years. Mr Lesland is the biological father of Caroline and is named on her birth certificate.

Mrs Lesland was in a previous relationship with Mr Thomas Gill (father of Rachel and Josh); however, this ended shortly after she became pregnant with Josh. Mrs Lesland was a single parent, working part time and managing the care of Rachel and Josh with the support of her mother, until Mr Lesland moved in with her 18 months ago. Mr Gill is not named on Rachel or Josh's birth certificates, he did not want to be as he incorrectly believed that this would mean Mrs Lesland would not be able to pursue him for financial support for the children if they separated.

Mrs Lesland does not know Mr Gill's whereabouts and he has not had contact with the children for about two years, coinciding with when Mrs Lesland met Mr Lesland.

Mr and Mrs Lesland's marital relationship has been deteriorating since the birth of Caroline. Mrs Lesland has been feeling low since Caroline's birth. Mrs Lesland's mother, Mrs Alice Price, was not very involved in Mrs Lesland's and the children's lives since Mrs Lesland married Mr Lesland. Mrs Price did not approve of the marriage as she believed that Mr Lesland was too old for her daughter.

Matters came to a head between Mr and Mrs Lesland, when Mr Lesland was caught by Mrs Lesland having an affair with her best friend, Sonia Payne, who is also godmother to Rachel and Josh.

Mrs Lesland was further devastated when she recently found out that Mr Lesland started his affair with Sonia Payne prior to her pregnancy with Caroline. The couple separated and Mr Lesland moved out of the family home. Mrs Lesland was left with the sole care of the children, and her situation became worse with the sudden death of her mother, Mrs Price. She feels isolated and lonely.

Mr Lesland, on leaving the marital home, had regular direct and telephone contact with the children for two months. Thereafter, Mrs Lesland terminated further contact as she felt that Mr Lesland could not manage all the children on his own during direct contact and that telephone contact was upsetting the older children.

Mr Lesland believed that the contact was stopped once Mrs Lesland found out that he was now cohabiting with Sonia Payne, having moved into her home. Mrs Lesland found this out when Mr Lesland reduced the payments he was making to her as he was now also making contributions to Sonia Payne's household expenses. Mrs Lesland works part time and was reliant on Mr Lesland's financial contributions. The financial reduction has had a substantial impact on her ability to meet all the household expenses, including rent.

Mr Lesland joined a support group for fathers who are denied contact with their children. He was advised by the group that Mrs Lesland was probably refusing contact due to "implacable hostility" and that she had no good reason to deny him contact and was only doing so due to her hostility towards him moving on with his life. Mr Lesland was also fearful that the children would be influenced by Mrs Lesland's hostility and was advised by the group that the children could develop "parental alienation syndrome". Mr Lesland wanted contact reinstated, sought legal advice and was considering private law family proceedings.

The Lesland case: Discussion

All children are vulnerable due to their age, immaturity and dependency on adults to care for them. When parents separate, this can place the children of the family in crisis and make them even more vulnerable to a range of social, financial, psychological, emotional and educational factors.

What are the concerns?

Based on the facts of this case study, the children are vulnerable in that they could be at risk of neglect due to their mother's low mood, financial impact due to the separation, and emotional impact due to the abrupt termination of Mr Lesland's contact.

Parental responsibility

Mrs Lesland has parental responsibility for all three children.

Mr Gill does not have parental responsibility for Rachel or Josh, but does have parental responsibility for Caroline by virtue of the fact that he was married to Mrs Lesland and also he is named on the birth certificate.

Although Mr Lesland does not have parental responsibility for Rachel or Josh, he is a significant person to them, given that he was part of the family household as a stepfather to them for the last two years.

Mrs Lesland's reasons for termination of the contact arrangements are based on welfare issues; no child protection issues have been raised. Even if Mrs Lesland is correct that Mr Lesland cannot manage all the children, depending on the older children's wishes, Mrs Lesland could have permitted Mr Lesland contact with the older children, including continuation of telephone contact.

Mr Lesland was having contact for the last two months; he certainly could consider his legal options to reinstate his contact with Caroline, and possibly the older children, depending on their wishes.

From the court's perspective, the fact that Mr Lesland has reduced his financial contributions is treated as a separate issue, unrelated to consideration for contact. Mrs Lesland should contact the Child Maintenance Service regarding his payments.

Private law proceedings

The Children Act 1989 covers both private and public law proceedings. Private law proceedings are legal proceedings between private individuals, such as family members who cannot agree on matters relating to a child's upbringing. These must be differentiated from public law proceedings, which are legal proceedings taken by or against the State. In children matters, public law proceedings are commenced by the local authority if a child is considered to be at risk of or has suffered significant harm.

In private law proceedings, an order can be sought under s. 8 of the Children Act 1989 by anyone who has an interest in or concern about a child's welfare. There is, however, a distinction between those who can apply as of right and those who must first seek permission of the court to make an application.

Children of sufficient understanding can seek leave of the court to make an application. However, the court will require a proper investigation as to the circumstances and whether the dispute can be resolved with the use of other methods. Parents are encouraged to resolve disputes without the need to commence legal proceedings. There are a number of ways in which this is achieved.

1 Presumption of parental involvement

Section 11 of the Children and Families Act 2014 introduced a statutory presumption of parental involvement, which has been inserted into a new section in the Children Act 1989 under welfare of the child:

s.2A Children Act 1989

A court...to presume, unless the contrary is shown, that involvement of that parent in the life of the child concerned will further the child's welfare.

s.2B Children Act 1989

"Involvement" means involvement of some kind, either direct or indirect, but not any particular division of a child's time.

This means that there is a presumption that children will benefit from the continuing relationship with both parents and that shared parenting is in the child's best interests. It also sends an important message to parents that they both play a valuable role in their child's life.

However, it should be noted that s.11 of the Children and Families Act 2014 does not create a presumption of shared parenting or equal division of time between the parents. This means that the presumption of parental involvement does not assume that parents are entitled to an equal share of the child's time when considering issues of contact or residence. However, as a starting position, the courts will apply the principle that both separated parents should continue to be involved in their children's lives, as long as it is safe to do so.

Another important point is that the presumption of parental involvement does not impact on the principle of parental responsibility and only affects the welfare principle enshrined in s.1 of the Children Act 1989; that is, the new inserted s.2A has the effect that, unless the contrary is shown, the court is to presume that the involvement of that parent in the child's life will further the child's welfare.

So when the court is dealing with an application relating to the child, the court starts with the presumption that involvement of that parent in the child's life will further the child's welfare. Therefore, the court will need to consider firstly whether a parent can be involved in the child's life in a way that does not impact on the child's welfare detrimentally. Section 2B of the Children Act 1989 clarifies that involvement does not mean an equal share of the child's time. Accordingly, the court then considers what form the contact should take, whether this is to be indirect or direct, and its duration and frequency.

2   Child arrangements orders

When parents cannot agree post separation on the future arrangements for a child, s.8 of the Children Act 1989 provides for orders that can be granted by the court if it considers that an order is necessary to promote and safeguard the child's welfare.

The Children and Families Act 2014 replaced residence and contact orders under s.8 of the Children Act 1989 with child arrangements orders. This order prescribes 'with whom a child is to live, spend time or otherwise have contact'. It therefore deals with both residence and contact issues[85] and concentrates on meeting the "needs" of the child and less on the "parental rights" over the child.

The change came about further to the recommendations of the Family Justice Review that set out two reasons for introducing this new order. Firstly, it was to encourage the parents or carers to be motivated to make their own suitable arrangements in relation to where the child is to live and with whom the child is to have contact; that if parents are unable to make their own arrangements, only then should they come to court to seek a child arrangements order. Secondly, by having only one type of order, it was hoped that the change in terminology would move away from the loaded terms "residency" and "contact" (as identified by the Family Justice Review) and help to eradicate the false view that being granted a residence order made the parent a "winner", and that if you were granted a contact order, you were a "loser". This was based on the mistaken belief that the party who was granted a residence order had attained all the rights to make decisions about the child as they were considered the primary parent, with the secondary parent being granted the contact order. The reform's intention was to create a more supportive approach and show that all parents are treated equally.

A child arrangements order means an order regulating arrangements relating to any of the following—

(a) with whom a child is to live, spend time or otherwise have contact, and

(b) when a child is to live, spend time or otherwise have contact with any person

85   S.12 Children and Families Act 2014

The starting point for any consideration of contact is that, unless it is not in the child's best interests, contact should be maintained. This was established in *M v M (Child Access)*,[86] when the Judge stated that contact is 'a basic right of the child'[87] to the companionship of their other parent. This judicial thinking has influenced the courts to the present day. The court's approach to contact is to favour it if the child will benefit from contact with the non-resident parent; that if an order for contact is necessary and important for the child's welfare, it should be granted.

3   Legal aid: Private law Children Act proceedings

There have been major legal aid cuts, which have resulted in very limited availability of legal aid for private law children proceedings. The Legal Aid, Sentencing and Punishment of Offenders Act 2012 made radical changes to the eligibility and availability of legal aid for private law children proceedings since April 2013. Legal aid is now not available in private law cases, unless the claimant falls within one of five exceptional categories:

- the applicant is a victim of domestic violence;

- the case involves a forced marriage injunction;

- the case involves allegations of child abuse;

- a child is party to the proceedings; or

- there are exceptional circumstances.

For a party to rely on one of the exemptions, evidence is required to support the category relied upon and the entitlement of the legal aid is means and merit tested. The solicitor instructed by the party will undertake the eligibility criteria as to whether the means and merit tests are met.

---

86 *M v M (Child Access)* [1973] 2 ALL ER 81

87 *M v M (Child Access)* [1973] 2 ALL ER 81, page 85

4   Mediation

If parents cannot reach agreement with regards to the arrangements for the child, then prior to making any application to court for a child arrangements order, they must first attend a Mediation Information and Assessment Meeting (MIAM).[88] This is a mandatory requirement and must be attended by the parents before any application is made to the court. Attendance is not applicable if there is evidence of domestic abuse or if any of the other exemptions listed above for entitlement to legal aid apply. MIAMs provide information and invite prospective litigants to consider mediation and other methods of alternative dispute resolution. The provision applies irrespective of whether the parties are privately funded or in receipt of legal aid.

Parties can apply for legal aid, as it can be available for MIAMs to one or both of the parties, with each party being assessed separately in order to consider financial eligibility for the entitlement. Therefore, parties who are facing attendance at a MIAM should discuss with their solicitor or the meditator their eligibility for legal aid and, if they are not eligible, they will have to meet the cost of the mediation meeting with the mediator prior to the first meeting.

If the MIAM is not successful in resolving the dispute, then proceedings can be commenced. The court will not consider any private law application unless it has received confirmation that a MIAM has been attempted.

For those individuals who are relying on one of the exemptions, MIAM attendance will not be necessary and proceedings can be commenced immediately.

The Lesland case: Discussion

The application of the presumption of parental involvement, that is, the benefit for the children from a continuing relationship with both parents, would support Mr Lesland in his desire to have contact reinstated with the children, given that he was having contact in the past and there are no child protection issues. This will support Mr Lesland in any application for a child arrangements order. However,

88 S.10 Children and Families Act 2014

before Mr Lesland considers any application to the court, he must consider the issue of funding for his legal representation. As this is a private law matter and as none of the exemption categories apply, he will not be entitled to legal aid in respect of his application for a child arrangements order, so he will have to fund payment of any legal advice and/or representation himself.

Both Mr and Mrs Lesland will be required to attend a MIAM appointment before commencement of an application to the court for a child arrangements order. If either refuses to attend, this is evidence that a MIAM was attempted.

Even though legal aid is not available for the application, it can be available for a MIAM appointment, so Mr and Mrs Lesland need to ascertain if they are financially eligible for legal aid to pay for their share of the MIAM appointment. This will be means-tested and both Mr and Mrs Lesland will need to be financially assessed.

The aim of the MIAM is to assist Mr and Mrs Lesland in reaching an agreement in relation to the children's contact arrangements, without recourse to any court application. Therefore, if agreement is reached, it will mean Mr Lesland will not need to apply to the court for a child arrangements order for contact between him and the children.

Throughout this process, there is no independent representation of the children. As part of the mediator's role, he or she will ask the parents to consider the impact of their actions on the children. However, the mediator does not meet the children and only receives information about the children from the parents.

---

5 The Lesland case: Part 2

Mr and Mrs Lesland attend the MIAM appointment. Mrs Lesland refuses to permit contact, stating that Mr Lesland cannot manage the care of Caroline and that the older children do not wish to see him as he is not their father.

Mr Lesland does not accept this; he states that he can manage the children, and that he used to care for them when Mrs Lesland went to work, and the contact went very well during the two months before it was stopped by Mrs Lesland. Mr

Lesland expresses to the mediator that it is his view that Mrs Lesland is being hostile and that her behaviour has resulted in the older children experiencing parental alienation syndrome, and that Mrs Lesland is doing this because she is jealous of his relationship with Sonia Payne. Mr Lesland states that if Mrs Lesland does not reinstate the contact, he will apply for a child arrangements order. He states that he knows he will not be eligible for legal aid for these proceedings and as he cannot afford the services of a solicitor, he will rely on the fathers' support group to assist him.

The Lesland case: Discussion

The MIAM appointment has been attended, and as a satisfactory resolution has not been achieved, Mr Lesland now proceeds with his application for a child arrangements order.

As Mr Lesland has parental responsibility for Caroline, he can make his application under s.8 of the Children Act 1989 in respect of her without leave (permission) of the court.

In relation to Rachel and Josh, as Mr Lesland does not have parental responsibility for them and has not lived with them for at least three years, he will need to apply for leave (permission) of the court before he can make his application. This means that he first needs to seek the court's permission to proceed with the substantive application for a child arrangements order. To do this, he will need to satisfy the relevant criteria listed in s.10(9) of the Children Act 1989:

> *Where the person applying for leave to make an application for a section 8 order is not the child concerned, the court shall, in deciding whether or not to grant leave, have particular regard to—*
>
> *(a) the nature of the proposed application for the section 8 order;*
>
> *(b) the applicant's connection with the child;*
>
> *(c) any risk there might be of that proposed application disrupting the child's life to such an extent that he would be harmed by it.*

The court, in deciding whether or not to grant leave, will take into account Mr Lesland's Articles 6 and 8 rights under the ECHR.

Mr Lesland's application for leave is likely to be successful as he can satisfy the above listed criteria; also, there is no evidence to suggest that his application is frivolous, vexatious or would be harmful to the children. In the leave application, Mr Lesland does not need to show he has a strong case in relation to his application for a child arrangements order.

If leave is granted, this does not mean that the substantive application for a child arrangements order will be successful.

Once Mr Lesland is granted leave, he can proceed with his substantive application.

---

6   Court welfare report

To assist the Judge, under s.7(1) of the Children Act 1989 the court is entitled to request an officer from CAFCASS to provide a report. This officer is called the family court reporter. Alternatively, the court can request a social worker from children's services to provide the report on matters relating to the child's welfare, as required, if the matter is open to children's services, or closed within the last 28 days, or if there are child protection issues raised by the parents.

The Lesland case: Discussion

Mr Lesland makes an application for Caroline and a leave application for the older children. Leave is granted and he also makes an application for a child arrangements order for the older children. Once the application is made, the parties are Mr and Mrs Lesland. The children do not have direct involvement in the proceedings and are dependent on the parents to either reach an agreement or the court to make a decision. The court may appoint an officer from CAFCASS or direct the child's social worker to provide the court with an independent welfare report that will include the children's views. In this case, as there has not been any involvement by children's services and as there are no child protection issues raised, it is likely that the court will request a family court reporter from CAFCASS to provide the welfare report.

Once the application is issued by the court, one of the first directions the court will consider making is under s.7 of the Children Act 1989:

7(1) A court considering any question with respect to a child under this Act may—

ask...an officer...to report to the court on such matters relating to the welfare of that child as are required to be dealt with in the report.

The family court reporter will seek the views of the parents at the first hearing and consider the issues in dispute, and whether a resolution can be achieved. The family court reporter's involvement will also be the first occasion on which an independent professional will seek the child's views by arranging to see them separately to their parents. The welfare report will record the child's wishes using the welfare checklist, as set out in s.1(3) of the Children Act 1989. The report's recommendations will set out the options available to the court and conclude by making a recommendation to the court that the report's author believes meets the child's best interests. Where there is a sibling group, the recommendations could differ; for example, for an older sibling, the author of the report may recommend unsupervised contact, whereas for the younger child, it may be preferable to have supervised contact until the child is older. The report's purpose is to assist the court in reaching their decision as to whether to grant a s.8 order.[89] Therefore, this report is highly influential on the court; however, should the court choose not to follow the recommendations, it must be prepared to justify the reason for its departure.

89 Children Act 1989

6.1 Children and Family Court Advisory and Support Service (CAFCASS)

CAFCASS was established by the Criminal Justice and Court Services Act 2000. It is a non-departmental body; it has a statutory responsibility in family proceedings to safeguard and promote the welfare of the children.

A CAFCASS officer/family court reporter is independent of children's services and other agencies, including health and education authorities. CAFCASS officers are appointed in both private and public law proceedings to independently represent the child's wishes and feelings and to ensure that their voice is heard in the family court. They can provide information, advice and other support to children and families and will make recommendations to the court which they consider necessary to safeguard and promote the child's welfare.

When making any recommendations to the court, the CAFCASS officer is required to have regard to the welfare checklist as set out in s.1(3) of the Children Act 1989. This includes the requirement to 'give due weight to the ascertainable wishes and feelings of the child concerned in the light of their age and understanding'.

The CAFCASS officer's role includes:

- explaining to the child independently about the options during the proceedings and the changes that may take place in their life;

- listening to the child, independently of their parents;

- helping the child to tell the court what they want;

- representing the child's views and interests in court;

- making recommendations that have the best possible outcomes for the child, having taken into account the views of the parties and the child.

To assist the CAFCASS officer, agencies, including children's services, are required to share relevant information that is necessary to assist the officer in their enquiries to promote the child's welfare.

In private law proceedings, if a CAFCASS officer or family court reporter is appointed, a check will be made as to whether the child is known to the local children's services department. The CAFCASS officer or family court reporter will also speak to the child's carers if the child is not in their parent's care, for example, if they are living with kinship carers.

A useful resource for children and those working or supporting children who are the subject of Children Act proceedings is the CAFCASS website: www.cafcass. gov.uk. This has a section for young people with helpful explanations of why families go to family courts, and CAFCASS's role. It also provides stories written by children who have experienced the process.

6.2   The local authority's involvement

If children's services has an open case for the child or if there are child protection concerns raised in the proceedings, in those circumstances the court can direct that the welfare report be prepared by children's services, and if there is an allocated social worker, can direct in the order that they prepare the report.

6.3   The child's voice

Children do not usually attend court and the child's views, wishes and feelings are brought to the court's attention in the welfare report. However, if a child wishes to meet the Judge, the court should be informed by the author of the welfare report. The Judge should also be advised whether the meeting will accord with the child's welfare. It is a matter for the Judge's discretion whether they agree to meet the child. If the Judge decides not to do so, as it is not considered to be in the child's best interests, then this should be explained to the child by the author of the welfare report. If the Judge decides to meet the child, the purpose of this meeting is not for them to gather evidence, as that is the responsibility of the author of the welfare report. The focus will be on enabling the child to gain some understanding of what is going on in the proceedings related to them and to be reassured that the Judge has understood them. In 2010, the Family Justice Council issued guidance on this which can be found at: https://bit.ly/2PoZOe0. This guidance was considered in the appeal case of Re KP (A Child).[90] In this case,

90   Re KP (A Child) [2014] EWCA Civ 554, [2014] 1 WLR 4326

it was emphasised that the child's meeting with the Judge is not for the purpose of gathering evidence (para 50).

On occasion, when dealing with complex cases, the court can consider the need for the child's voice to be directly part of the proceedings. This may be necessary where the Judge forms the view that the parties are unable to make a decision based on the child's best interests. Rule 16.2 of the Family Procedure Rules 2010 allows the court to make a child a party to an application and to be separately represented. This will enable the court to hear the child's views directly in the proceedings through the independent representation of a Children's Guardian appointed from CAFCASS and from the solicitor appointed for the child.

6.4 The Lesland case: Part 3

Once the application for a child arrangements order was issued by the court, the family court reporter from CAFCASS was appointed. They made various visits to the parents and children. As part of their investigation, they considered the issues raised by Mr and Mrs Lesland, including Mr Lesland's view about the level of Mrs Lesland's hostility towards him and the negative impact of this on the children by alienating them from having a relationship with him.

7 Implacable hostile parent

Implacable hostility is where a parent opposes the child having contact with the other parent for no justifiable reason, and develops hostility towards promoting contact with that parent. If the court is faced with a parent objecting to contact, the reasons for this will need to be fully investigated by the family court reporter or social worker. If it is considered to be in the child's best interests, the court can grant a child arrangements order,[91] ordering the hostile parent to make the child available for contact.

91 S.8 Children Act 1989

The Children and Adoption Act 2006[92] gives the courts powers to promote and enforce child arrangements orders directing contact. The underlying aim of the Act is to encourage the non-co-operative parent to comply with the order. Therefore, where a child arrangements order directing contact has not been complied with, this Act inserts new sections into the Children Act 1989 which enable the court to take steps to support the implementation of the order and to help the resident parent to comply with it. To achieve this, the court can make directions and if necessary step up to coercive measures,[93] such as:

- the power to impose contact activity directions and conditions. This could include either or both parties attending counselling or guidance programmes to help to establish, maintain or improve the life of the child or another individual;

- the power, in certain circumstances, to order that a person should be compensated for financial loss incurred as a result of a breach of the child arrangements order;

- the power to require CAFCASS to monitor contact;[94]

- the power to attach a warning notice of the consequences of not complying with the child arrangements order;[95]

- the power to make an enforcement order, imposing on the person an unpaid work requirement.[96]

8 Parental alienation syndrome

This is where the resident parent is said to turn the child against the non-resident parent. In *Re S (Transfer of Residence)*,[97] the syndrome was accepted to exist

92 This came into force on 8 December 2008.
93 Ss.11A–11P Children Act 1989, inserted by the Children and Adoption Act 2006
94 Inserts into the Children Act 1989, s.11H
95 Inserts into the Children Act 1989, s.11I
96 Inserts into the Children Act 1989, s.11J–N
97 *Re S (Transfer of Residence)* [2010] 1 FLR 1785

by the Court of Appeal. It is important to note that it is not always the case that simply because a child is objecting to having contact with a non-resident parent, that is attributed to the syndrome. In the case of *Re C (Children: Contact)*,[98] the Judge's view was that the children's refusal to have contact with the non-resident father was more likely to do with the fact that he had left his wife and children for another woman, rather than due to parental alienation syndrome.

However, in cases where parental alienation is found, it can be harmful to the child. It can also be difficult for the court to rely on the child's wishes and feelings, given that they may be unreliable as the child could be expressing the view of their parent. It is therefore important for the professionals involved to understand fully the history of the case, as was identified in the case of *Re D*,[99] which involved parents who had been embroiled in court proceedings on and off since 2008, relating to their son D (who in 2018 was 13 years old).

In 2016, D, who lived with his father, started having increased contact with his mother, with the father's agreement. During this period, the school made a child protection referral to the effect that D was frightened of his father. On further investigation, no evidence was found to support this. The mother then applied for the residence of D to be transferred to her, with a child arrangements order to be made in her favour. The father objected, and requested the court to make a finding that the mother had alienated D from him.

The Judge found that the mother had deliberately alienated the child from his father, driven by her desire for D to live with her.

This case had a long history, and one of the criticisms of the social worker who had undertaken the s.37 investigation was that she had failed 'to acquaint herself adequately with the relevant background papers' (para 209). There had been previous hearings where the Judges involved had rejected allegations by the mother of violence by the father, including rape of the mother and abuse of D. The Judge went on to say that the social worker 'when undertaking the s.37 investigation was completely unaware of those observations and findings' made in these previous hearings (para 209). This meant that the social worker's

98 *Re C (Children: Contact)* [2002] 3 FCR 183, [2002] 1 FLR 1136
99 *Re D* [2018] EWFC B 64

current assessment was flawed and, combined with her lack of knowledge and experience in the area of parental alienation, meant that the 'judgements she has reached become highly questionable'. This case highlights important points for those professionals who may be involved in these types of cases, that is, to be familiar with the full history of the case and the research in this area.

One of the other consequences of the parents' battle in the *Re D* case, as noted by the Judge, was that as the parents were not entitled to legal aid, as their finances exceeded the means test, they both funded the case from their own private funds. The father had spent in excess of £200,000, and the mother had spent £120,000. The Judge concluded that: 'this is an eye-watering amount of money to spend in a battle to win the heart and mind of a child. These parents need to invest their resources in trying to undo the immense harm that has been caused to this very likeable young man' (para 260).

The case of *Re H C (Parental Alienation)*[100] is another where there had been continuous court proceedings since the parents' separation, in 2007. This was the sixth set of proceedings in relation to H (a 12-year-old child), who lived with her mother and enjoyed regular contact with her father and the paternal family until March 2018, when it abruptly stopped.

The Judge found that the mother had repeatedly lied in her evidence and used any opportunity to blame the father; and concluded that she had alienated H from her father. The Judge ordered that residence of H transfer to the father, as that was the only means by which H could enjoy a relationship with him, the absence of which would cause H emotional and social harm. The court made a child arrangements order to the father, and added a three month embargo on contact for the mother. This was considered necessary to allow time for H to settle.

9   Section 37 reports

Where there are private law proceedings and the Judge is concerned about the child's welfare, the Judge can direct under s.37 of the Children Act 1989 the local authority to investigate the child's circumstances and consider whether the

---

100 *Re H C (Parental Alienation)* [2019] EWAC 2723 (Fam)

authority should apply for a care or supervision order, or whether to offer any services:

> *s.37(1) Where, in any family proceedings in which a question arises with respect to the welfare of any child, it appears to the court that it may be appropriate for a care or supervision order to be made with respect to him, the court may direct the appropriate authority to undertake an investigation of the child's circumstances.*

The court will require the report to be provided within eight weeks from the date of the direction, unless the court otherwise directs.

If the local authority, having undertaken its investigation, decides not to apply for a care or supervision order, then the report must include:

> *(a) their reasons for so deciding;*
>
> *(b) any service or assistance which they have provided, or intend to provide, for the child and his family; and*
>
> *(c) any other action which they have taken, or propose to take, with respect to the child.*

It is advisable for the social worker preparing the report to seek legal advice before filing it, so that it includes clear analysis of the information as to whether the local authority considers that the threshold criteria for issuing care or supervision order proceedings have been met, and, if not, to include why the local authority consider that the threshold criteria have not been met and, if appropriate, what support can be offered.

Case study 4: Cross allegations

In this case, a mother and father had separated, and could not reach agreement as to the arrangements for their six-year-old son. The mother sought a child arrangements order for the child to live with her; this was opposed by the father, who wanted the child to live with him.

In the proceedings, the mother alleged that the father was an alcoholic, and that during contact he used the child to distract shop owners so that he could steal bottles of alcohol. The father denied the allegations and made a cross-allegation that the mother was a drug dealer, that she had CCTV cameras all over her property and that their son was at great risk if he continued to live with her.

The Judge in these private law proceedings became extremely concerned as to the child's welfare and directed the local authority to undertake a s.37 investigation as to whether care proceedings should be commenced.

The social worker concluded that she could not find any evidence to support either parent's allegations, and that this was an extremely acrimonious couple. To support the child, the local authority formulated a "child in need" plan. The local authority clarified that it would not issue care proceedings; however, it would continue to be involved, would keep the "child in need" plan under review, and, if necessary, would provide additional support. The court then directed a s.7 welfare report to the cross applications for the child arrangements order.

---

10   The Lesland case: Part 4

The family court reporter completed his investigation and a s.7 welfare report. As part of his investigation, he spoke to Rachel and Josh alone; they both stated that they did not want to have contact with Mr Lesland as they felt that he has always prioritised Caroline and made them feel that they are not his children. They were also extremely upset by his departure from the family home.

In order to ascertain what would meet Caroline's needs, the family court reporter observed contact between Mr Lesland and Caroline, which was positive. The family court reporter recognised that Mr Lesland did struggle when feeding Caroline and changing her nappy.

The recommendations of the family court reporter were that direct contact with Caroline and Mr Lesland should be resumed; also, given her young age and Mr Lesland's limitations in meeting all her needs, that the contact should take place at Mr Lesland's mother's home. This would allow the paternal grandmother to support Mr Lesland at feeding and nappy changing times. The recommended frequency was to be once every fortnight on a Saturday morning for two hours. This would enable Caroline to also have contact with her paternal grandmother, who would be available to support Mr Lesland, if necessary.

The family court reporter did not find any evidence of implacable hostility or parental alienation syndrome and accepted that the older children's views as provided were their own. The family court reporter recommended that Mr Lesland could have indirect contact by sending cards and letters to Rachel and Josh once a month, and that should they wish to speak to Mr Lesland, he could have contact by telephone with them once a fortnight. It was the family court reporter's view that over time Rachel and Josh may change their views and could join the same contact with Caroline.

Mrs Lesland did not support the family court reporter's recommendations and opposed the making of a child arrangements order.

Having heard from both parents and taking into account the family court reporter's report, the court grants a child arrangements order for contact for all three children in accordance with the family court reporter's recommendations.

5

The family and local authority

The provision of services by children's services is a broad local authority function. Services can range from provision of information and services from early years nursery and toddler groups to education services or facilities for young people under 18. Children's services do not do this alone and can seek the support of other agencies within and outside the local authority in carrying out these functions.

1   Co-operation between authorities

Section 27 of the Children Act 1989 places a specific duty on local authority services and health bodies to co-operate in the interests of children in need:

> *s.27(1) Where it appears to a local authority that any authority...could, by taking any specified action, help in the exercise of any of their functions... they may request the help of that other authority...specifying the action in question.*

> *s.27(2) An authority whose help is so requested shall comply with the request if it is compatible with their own statutory or other duties and obligations and does not unduly prejudice the discharge of any of their functions.*

Therefore, children's services can request assistance from other authorities, including any other local authority, local housing authority, local education authority, or health authority.

This statutory provision was further strengthened by ss.10 and 11 of the Children Act 2004, which place a duty on local authorities to make arrangements for promoting co-operation to improve children's well-being.

2   The Lesland case: Part 5

On the making of the child arrangements order, Mrs Lesland's health deteriorates. Mrs Lesland goes to her GP; she has lost her appetite, and sleeps long hours. She also leaves her job. The GP's view is that Mrs Lesland is suffering from depression, and she is prescribed anti-depressants.

Shortly after the child arrangements order was granted, Mr Lesland is offered a job abroad and decides to take it. Since leaving the UK, he has not maintained any indirect contact by letter or phone with the children. He informs Mrs Lesland that he will have to stop any financial payments as he will need the money to pay for his travel and accommodation abroad.

Rachel and Josh's class teachers are concerned that the children often arrive late for the start of school; they frequently appear tired and Josh has fallen asleep in class. When asked why he is tired, Josh tells his teacher that he is constantly hungry and as a result finds it difficult to sleep. He further says that since their step-father left, they do not have breakfast as their mother is sleeping, and that she has not been for a "proper shop", and the cereal finished "ages ago".

A meeting is set up by the school safeguarding lead with Mrs Lesland. She admits that she is often struggling to meet the children's needs and acknowledges that she requires support.

Further to discussion with the school safeguarding lead, the head agrees to fund breakfast club for the children. Rachel attends but Josh often does not. Rachel says that this is because their mother does not get Josh ready in time and Josh will not listen to Rachel.

Within a few weeks of the provision of breakfast club, the situation worsens. Josh tells his class teacher that there have been a few times when he and Rachel have drunk Vimto and eaten biscuits for dinner. Both class teachers report that at times the children come to school without a packed lunch and the school catering staff have had to provide them with lunch.

The children's school attendance becomes very poor. When they do attend, their appearance is of concern, and they have unwashed clothes. Rachel is upset as her friends no longer want to play with her, as they say she smells and has head lice.

Rachel tells her teacher that she is worried Caroline is not being fed until Rachel gets home from school, and that there is sometimes no food in the house as her mother has not gone shopping. Rachel's teacher passes the information to the school safeguarding lead who then attempts to speak to Mrs Lesland on several occasions, but she does not answer her phone. As a result of the increasing concerns relating to Rachel, Josh and Caroline, the school safeguarding lead makes a referral to children's services.

---

3   Referrals

From a child's perspective, the earlier support and/or assistance is provided, the better. Professionals, family, friends or members of the public can make referrals to children's services if there are concerns about any child's welfare. If a professional makes a referral, good practice is that they should detail the referral in writing, clearly recording the concerns about the child's welfare and what action they have taken to date.

On receipt of the referral, children's services can decide to:

- provide advice or information or signpost the referrer;
- make an onward referral to another agency for provision of services;
- commence an initial assessment of the child's needs; or
- take no further action.

Once a referral is received by children's services, a decision will be made as to how it will be actioned. A written record will be made of the decision, reasons for the action and who will be taking the action. Good practice is that, if the referrer is a professional, feedback of this information should be given. Should the decision be that the concerns do not meet the threshold for intervention by children's services, feedback to the referrer should also include any suggestions for other sources of more suitable support. If an update or satisfactory response is not received from children's services, the professional who made the referral should always follow up their concerns and enquire what action has been taken.

Information is shared, maintaining the duty of confidentiality to the child and family. All information is recorded in the child's file, held by children's services.

When children's services makes the decision to act upon a referral and become involved in a child's case, four key processes are undertaken in all cases:

- Assessment
- Care planning
- Intervention or not
- Review of the care plan

Refer to Flowchart 1, which details the referral process and the different avenues the referral can lead to.

4 Assessments

When children's services decides to take action following a referral, it commences the process by undertaking an assessment. The process will start with an initial assessment, during which information is gathered using the assessment framework triangle model (see Appendix 1), which examines the three different aspects of the child's life: the child's development needs, the child's parents'/carers' parenting capacity, and the child's family and environmental factors, and how each of these areas impact on the child.

When undertaking the initial assessment, the child's social worker will undertake:

- gathering of information about the child and family;

- an analysis of the needs of the child and/or their family and the nature and level of any risk of harm to the child;

- further to the analysis, children's services will decide what action to take.

Following the initial assessment, the child's social worker will undertake a more in-depth assessment known as the children and family assessment. The purpose of this is to consider the key aspects of the needs of the child and their parents' or carers' ability to meet those needs, and to consider what support is required to improve the child's welfare.

- If the child is assessed to be a child in need, a child in need plan will be formulated and services will be provided under s.17 of the Children Act.

- If the child is assessed as being at risk of significant harm or likely to suffer significant harm, a decision will need to be made whether to commence a child protection investigation under s.47 of the Children Act or to commence legal proceedings.

The importance of assessments was highlighted in the case of *Re Z (Child: Independent Social Work Assessments)* para 130,[101] where the Judge stated:

> *In any case in which a local authority applies to the court for a care order, the assessment of a parent is of critical importance. That assessment will be a key piece of the evidential jigsaw which informs the local authority's decision-making, in particular with respect to the formulation of its care plan. If the assessment is deficient, that is likely to undermine the reliability of the decision-making process. It follows, therefore, that any assessment of a parent must be, and must be seen to be, fair, robust and thorough.*

---

101 *Re Z (Child: Independent Social Work Assessments)* [2014] EWHC 729 (Fam)

Flowchart 1: Initial referral

This flowchart details the different routes an initial referral can lead to within children's services.

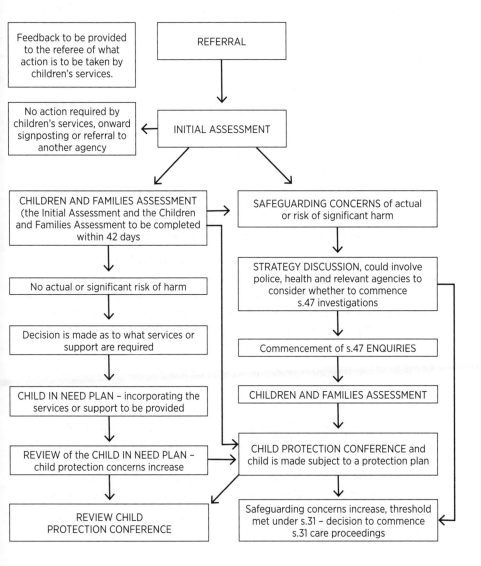

The Lesland case: Discussion

The school, having concerns about Rachel and Josh, initially attempted to put support in place. This was not sufficient and, futher to the children telling their teachers of their home situation, the safeguarding lead followed the correct procedure as set out in *Working Together to Safeguard Children* (DfE, 2015) by contacting children's services and making a referral. On receipt, and having undertaken an initial assessment, children's services could:

- take no action; or

- offer the school advice on how the children could be further supported by the school or other agencies; or

- undertake a fuller children and families assessment to assess whether the children require support and/or services.

Given that the concerns are of a nature that do potentially place the children as children in need, in this case action would need to be taken by children's services with the commencement of a children and family assessment.

There can be a tendency at times for professionals to focus on the support that the parents require at the earlier stages of intervention. In many cases, it may be absolutely reasonable to support the parent, to enable them to improve their parenting capacity. Professionals will be more able to support a co-operative parent who is accepting of services and support. However, it is important for professionals to remain child-focused and not be distracted by parents' needs.

One way in which supporting professionals can maintain the focus on the child would be to ensure that the child's voice is heard through the early assessment process. This will assist the professional to fully assess the child's needs, which in turn will enable the professional to ascertain what level of support the child requires or what form of support the parent requires to meet the child's needs. This process is supported by s.17(4A) of the Children Act 1989,[102] which requires local authorities, where practicable, to take account of the child's wishes and feelings before determining what services to provide or what action to take.

102 As amended by s.53(1) Children Act 2004.

5   Children in need

Section 17 of the Children Act 1989 places on the local authority the duty to provide appropriate services for children in need:

s.17 Provision of services for children in need, their families and others.

(1) It shall be the general duty of every local authority (in addition to the other duties imposed on them by this Part)—

(a) to safeguard and promote the welfare of children within their area who are in need; and

(b) so far as is consistent with that duty, to promote the upbringing of such children by their families, by providing a range and level of services appropriate to those children's needs.

Section 17(11) defines "development" to mean physical, intellectual, emotional, social and behavioural development, and "health" to mean physical or mental health.

Section 17 places a general duty on the local authority to promote and safeguard the welfare of children in need in their area. This is in line with the least interventionist approach, by providing services that may, over time, reduce or eliminate the need for the child to be brought into care, if the support provided meets their needs.

Services can be provided to the child or their family, which includes anyone with parental responsibility, and any person with whom the child is or has been living.

It is for children's services to determine whether a child is in need and what services are required. In order to determine this, children's services will undertake an assessment of need. If the assessment concludes that services are required, they will be provided with a view to safeguarding or promoting the child's welfare. The services can be provided to the child, children or the family as a whole and may include giving assistance in kind or even in cash, for example, the provision of short-term accommodation to the family.

This duty gives the local authority flexibility in providing the right support as and when, and for how long, it is required. However, any support offered will be dependent on the identified assessed need of the child. Further consideration will first be given as to whether that need can be provided by any other resource, including family and friends support.

Section 17 of the Children Act 1989 permits the local authority to make cash payments to children in need and their families,[103] and there no longer have to be exceptional circumstances. This allows the local authority to exercise a wider discretion over the circumstances in which they can make cash payments to those caring for children in need. This can enable the authority to provide regular and continuing financial support to children in need where this is assessed as being the most appropriate way to safeguard and promote their welfare.

It should be noted that in these cash-strapped times for local authorities, provision of services or financial support will often require senior management approval before the service or finances are authorised and provided.

The local authority also has the power to charge for services provided under s.17 of the Children Act 1989. Before it does this, it will take into account the family's means. If the local authority decides to charge, it can charge what it perceives to be a "reasonable sum", and not the actual cost of the service.

6   Disabled children

All children with disabilities are regarded as children in need under s.17(10)(c). Section 17(11) of the Children Act 1989 defines a child as disabled if they are impaired visually, have hearing or speech difficulties, suffer from a mental disorder of any kind (all of which require medical evidence), or are substantially and permanently disabled by illness, injury or congenital deformity or other such disability as may be prescribed.

Simply because a child is recognised as disabled and falls within the definition of disability as set out in s.17(11), this does not make the child automatically eligible for children in need services. The children's disability team will undertake

103 S.17(6) Children Act 1989

an assessment, firstly to consider whether the child's needs cross their service's threshold for services. If the team accepts that the threshold is crossed, the child will be eligible for an assessment of needs, and if a service is to be provided, they will be allocated a social worker.

The provision of services to children with disabilities is further supplemented by Schedule 2 to the Children Act 1989, paragraph 6(1):

> (1) Every local authority shall provide services designed—
>
>> (a) to minimise the effect on disabled children within their area of their disabilities;
>>
>> (b) to give such children the opportunity to lead lives which are as normal as possible; and
>>
>> (c) to assist individuals who provide care for such children to continue to do so, or to do so more effectively, by giving them breaks from caring.

This duty under paragraph 6(1)(c) of Schedule 2 of the Children Act is often known as the "short breaks duty". The local authority must provide a range of short break services, including respite, to be offered to families caring for children, including children with disabilities, following an assessment that identifies this as a need. This service is in the form of short-term pre-planned substitute care provided by preferably the same carer who is not the child's parent or usual carer. It can include:

- day care for the child with the disability, which could be in the home or externally;

- provision of overnight care for the child with the disability in their own home or elsewhere;

- provision for the child with the disability to participate in educational or recreational activities; and

- emergency care that may be required, due to illness within the family or safeguarding reasons (DfE, 2011, p 10).

The provision of this service enables the parents or carers of the child with disabilities to have some free time to allow them to rest or spend time with their other children. It can be arranged as a one-off, on a regular basis, and at times on an emergency basis. The duty to provide short breaks can be offered by the local authority through the use of s.17 or s.20 of the Children Act 1989.

If services are provided under s.17(6) of the Children Act 1989, this enables the local authority to provide accommodation as part of a range of services in order to discharge its general duty to safeguard and promote the child's welfare. If services are provided under this section, a "child in need" plan will be formulated by the child's social work team, detailing the services that are to be offered to the child. This provision of service will not mean that the child is treated as being looked after by the local authority. The child will not be allocated an Independent Reviewing Officer (IRO); however, the "child in need" plan will be reviewed by children's services at least every six months, or more often, if necessary.

Accommodation for short breaks can also be provided under s.20(4) of the Children Act 1989, which gives the local authority the ability to provide accommodation to any child in their area (even though a person who has parental responsibility for the child is able to provide them with accommodation) if they consider that to do so would safeguard or promote the child's welfare.

The local authority needs to be clear on what legal basis it is providing the service, and this will be determined by assessment of the child's needs, the wishes and feelings of the child and those of the child's parents or carers, their parenting capacity, and the wider family and environmental factors.

If accommodation is provided under s.20 for short breaks of more than 17 consecutive days per placement or more than 75 days in a 12-month period, then the child is treated as a child who is looked after for the period that they are provided with accommodation, and will be eligible for all the services for children who are looked after. This will include regular reviews by the IRO. The local authority must draw up a short break care plan addressing issues key to the child's safe care.

6.1   Continuity of support for disabled children

If a disabled child is receiving support from a children's disability social care team, then s.67 of the Care Act 2014 stipulates that the assessments of the child undertaken before they became 18 will continue to apply when they become 18 and until the assessment is reviewed by adult services. If adult services does not treat the assessments as a continuing obligation, then it must reassess. This provision ensures that there is no gap in the services provided to the young person on their 18th birthday, simply because responsibility for them is moving from the children's disability team to adult services.

---

7   The Lesland case: Part 6

Due to the nature of the referral to children's services, in particular, concerns relating to Caroline, children's services decide to commence a "child in need" assessment for all three children under s.17 of the Children Act 1989.

Josh has learning difficulties and was diagnosed as being on the autistic spectrum. He does not meet the threshold for services from the children with disabilities team. The children are allocated a children's social worker from the "children in need" team. A children and family assessment is commenced.

The social worker speaks to Mrs Lesland, who confirms that finances have been very tight since she left work and that Mr Lesland had stopped all financial support. This had resulted in a reduction in the purchase of the family groceries, but she is adamant that she does feed her children.

The social worker requests permission to speak to Caroline's health visitor and the children's GP; Mrs Lesland agrees. The health visitor and GP have concerns about Mrs Lesland's mental health. The health visitor is also concerned that Caroline is lacking stimulation, as she appears to be left for long periods in her bouncer.

As part of the assessment, the social worker decides to convene a family group conference to consider what support is available to Mrs Lesland and the children.

The children's social worker devises a "child in need" plan, requiring Mrs Lesland to ensure that Rachel and Josh continue to attend the breakfast club, and signposts her to a food bank.

Mrs Lesland agrees to send the children to breakfast club, but refuses to go to the food bank as she has never done this and does not want to start. She is referred to the welfare benefit rights officer to ensure that she is receiving all the welfare benefits she is entitled to.

The social worker requests Mr Lesland's contact details. Mrs Lesland only has his mobile phone number, which she says had been disconnected some time ago, and has no other contact details for him.

8   Children's social workers

Social work operates within a framework of legislation, Government guidance and local authority processes. Children's social workers have a general duty to consider ways of supporting or resolving challenges for children and families in difficult times to enable effective change. As mentioned previously, social workers should try to work in partnership with parents. They will endeavour to do this by engaging in non-judgemental and open communication, building trust in a sensitive way, taking into account the child's and family's ethnicity, religion, culture and language. The child's social worker will form a relationship with the child and family and gather information. This will help them to use their professional judgement to assess how best to work with the child and parents and what support is required to promote change in the parents so that they can meet their child's welfare and needs.

The child remains central throughout this process. The social worker is appointed as the child's social worker even though they may be working with the family to bring about sustainable positive changes. In the exercise of their role, the social worker has to achieve a fine balance of supporting the parents to meet their child's needs and ensuring that the child's welfare is safeguarded.

Child protection professionals are constantly making judgements that impinge on the rights of parents to be with and relate to their children and the parallel right of children to their parents. The stakes are high and child protection decision-making needs to be as explicit as possible and be available for review and scrutiny.

(Turnell, in press)

Children's social workers are experts in their field, as they are trained to understand children's development and their developing needs. They gather information and evidence by undertaking assessments to ascertain the child's needs and to consider what services are required to meet them. They work in a multi-agency environment and liaise closely with other agencies connected to the child. It is no easy task, particularly if they are faced with a situation in which they need to make professional judgements in a short space of time. A well publicised example is the social worker who visited Baby P (Peter Connolly) and found him with a chocolate-covered face. She asked for his face to be washed, whereupon he was taken by a family friend to be cleaned up. The social worker did not request to see the child once his face was washed. If she had, then she would have observed the facial bruising that had been disguised by the chocolate. In hindsight, it seems obvious that the social worker should have requested to see the child's clean face. However, at the time, how many social workers would have done this? It is a question of judgement, the social worker did not suspect that the smeared chocolate was covering up abuse. The mother was co-operative, and appeared compliant by giving access to her home and the child. Social work practice requires expertise, patience and the ability to make sound professional judgements. This was recognised by the Social Work Task Force (2010):

Helping children, families and adults who are in crisis or in difficult or dangerous situations to be safe, to cope and take control of their lives again requires exceptional professional judgment. Social workers have to be highly skilled in their interactions and must draw on a sound professional understanding of social work. They have to be able to do all of this while sustaining strong partnerships with the children or adults they are working with and their families: sometimes they will be the only people offering the stability and consistency that is badly needed.

The work of a social worker is not without its challenges, but equally the impact of their work can result in far-reaching and life-changing improvements in the child's and/or the family's circumstances.

Case study 5: Social workers do change lives

Yasmin had been trafficked into the UK a few years ago, when she was probably eight or nine. She had been living with a family who were using her as a domestic servant; she did not attend school and was kept hidden in the family home.

Agencies became aware of Yasmin after she was brought to the Accident and Emergency department of the local hospital by a man from this same family who claimed to be her private foster carer. He stated that she had stomach pains, which he believed to be the onset of her menstrual cycle. Yasmin did not speak English and therefore could not provide any further explanation for her pains. On medical examination, it transpired that Yasmin's stomach ache was due to the fact that she was in the late stages of pregnancy and was in labour. A few hours later, she gave birth to a premature baby boy. When asked, Yasmin did not know how old she was. This is not unusual in some communities where birthdays are not celebrated. After taking a bone density test, it was estimated that Yasmin was probably 13 or 14.

Care proceedings were commenced immediately in relation to Yasmin, her baby and the other children living in the family's household. Yasmin and the baby were placed in a parent and child foster placement. Despite her young age, Yasmin was observed to be very attentive to the baby's needs, and it was clear that, despite her young age, she had good parenting skills, no doubt acquired from her years of supporting the care of the younger children in the household. The care plan in the care proceedings was for Yasmin to remain in long-term foster care. It was explained to Yasmin that, in relation to her baby, should she wish to continue to parent, her baby could remain with her in care in a supportive foster placement, until Yasmin reached the age of 18. If she did not want that, the baby could be placed for adoption.

With the support of her devoted social worker, Yasmin made a very brave and difficult decision. She stated that she loved her baby and that if she had been older would have continued to care for him; however, given her age and lack of education, she felt it was best if her baby was adopted. Yasmin felt that it was better for her baby to be cared for by a two-parent family who could provide a better future for him. Her wish for herself was to go to school, to learn English. It was her hope to train to be a social worker, motivated by the way in which her own social worker had changed her life, so she could help others to change their lives for the better in the future.

Yasmin suffered a horrendous beginning to her life; she suffered sexual, emotional and physical abuse from the people whom she had been sent to live with. However, despite this she remained extremely optimistic about her future, and attributed this to her social worker. Yasmin's social worker had played a key part in communicating with her, helping her to understand the processes, keeping her informed, listening to her, and supporting her. Yasmin was a girl who had no experience of the world outside the family's home in which she worked. She had not been to school; she spoke no English; and was very fearful of the authorities and professionals involved in her and her baby's life. The positive relationship with her social worker helped her to build trust with the professionals around her and her baby. Yasmin was encouraged by her social worker to have a voice, to be listened to, and for her views to be acted upon in formulating her own care plan and in progressing her baby's care plan.

Yasmin remained in foster care and her baby was eventually adopted by a two-parent family. Yasmin asked to meet the adopters and, despite this being a very difficult meeting, told them the baby's likes and dislikes and her experiences of him when he was born, so that the adopters could share this with the baby when he was older as part of his life story. It was agreed that Yasmin would have "letter-box" contact twice a year, when she would send letters to her baby and the adopters would write to Yasmin informing her of the child's progress.

I met Yasmin's social worker a few years after this case was concluded. She was no longer Yasmin's social worker but had heard from her current social worker that Yasmin was still progressing with her education and her plans to one day become a social worker.

9 Family group conferences

Based on the presumption that the best place for a child is within their family, and on the basis of the least interventionist approach, the local authority should ascertain at a very early stage of involvement who else in the family or friends network may be able to support the parents in caring for their child or be potential carers for the child. In order to progress this process, children's social workers will request the parents to provide names of family members or significant persons connected to the family who can be part of a family group conference (FGC).

FGCs are a decision-making and planning process, led by the family and friends network to consider how the child's welfare is to be promoted or safeguarded. They were first developed in New Zealand after concerns were raised around the disproportionate number of Maori children in care and placed with white families. In New Zealand, FGCs are convened as the first step for planning and making decisions relating to children's welfare.

Until the introduction, in England and Wales in 2008, of the original Public Law Outline (PLO), the case management system applicable to cases where care or supervision order proceedings are being considered, FGCs were used in an *ad hoc* way. Some local authorities had very formalised processes for FGCs in place, whereas others used them on a case-by-case basis, and some did not use them at all. With the introduction of the PLO, many local authorities began to adopt a model of convening an FGC at an early stage of the authority's intervention. This provides an opportunity for children's services to engage with wider family members and friends, to consider how they could support the parents in the care of their child, or provide short-term care. It also invites family members to be considered as long-term carers in the event that the assessment of the parents is not positive and the child cannot remain in or return to the parents' care.

Early use of FGCs is considered to be an effective process prior to commencement of care proceedings, and recognised as providing an important opportunity to engage parents and family members in the discussion about the child's future care. This was accepted and formed one of the Public Law Working Group's recommendations (2020, p 32, para 49):

Effective pre-proceedings work, including FGCs (or a similar model for engaging with the family) being considered as a matter of routine and the use of the Family Rights Group's Initial Family and Friends Care Assessment: A good practice guide, (endorsed by the Family Justice Council and CAFCASS) should enable early identification of those family or friend carers who are a realistic option to care for the child. This should avoid scenarios where significant resources are devoted to lengthy assessment of numerous individuals who are not a realistic option for the child.

Other models separate to the formal FGC process have been developed, such as family network meetings. In essence, the purpose is the same. Whatever model is used, it is important that the meeting is convened as early as possible to assist with the care planning process. The meeting assists the family/friends network to understand the concerns and to consider what support they can offer. The major benefit is that it can reduce or even possibly eliminate the need for the child to become looked after and placed in local authority care, such as foster care. This is again in line with the least interventionist approach of the Children Act 1989; that is, to keep the child within their family, and respect both the child's and family's Article 8 rights. Should it be necessary, family or friends placement may also mean that care proceedings do not need to be commenced, as the child will be in a protective environment whilst the local authority undertakes assessments of the parents.

The term "family" for the purposes of an FGC is widely defined and can include non-blood relatives and significant others. It can also include friends or anyone who is significant to the child (also known as connected persons), including an advocate for the child. Families should be encouraged to include as many family members and friends as possible in the FGC process.

Consideration should be given to inviting fathers, irrespective of whether they have parental responsibility or not, and their families. If there are concerns in relation to domestic abuse, possible conflict in family dynamics or information sharing that could interfere with the smooth running of an FGC, consideration should be given to holding the meeting in two parts to avoid possible conflict. The process will need to be managed by the co-ordinator (FGC) or the social worker in family network meetings, who will first gather the information from the child's social worker.

There are four key stages of the FGC process:

- **Consent**

  Once a decision has been made to convene an FGC, the child's social worker will seek signed written consent from those who have parental responsibility to agree to a referral for an FGC, to contact family and friends, and for the information to be shared at the FGC with the family members.

  In cases where parents refuse to provide consent to contact family members or refuse to provide information to enable the child's social worker to invite family members to an FGC, if proceedings have already commenced, the local authority can seek appropriate court directions or approval of its care plan. If proceedings have not commenced, then due to data protection constraints, children's social workers cannot override parents' wishes. In good practice guidance, the Public Law Working Group has recommended that further clarity is required from the Information Commissioner of circumstances where it would be acceptable to override lack of consent (2019, para 92).

  With the parents' consent, the child's social worker will then make a referral to the FGC service. The service can be provided either by the local authority directly or by external services. Whichever is used, it is independent of the children's social work team. An independent FGC co-ordinator is appointed who will meet with the child's social worker and thereafter the family members and friends (participants) who have been identified by the family. The co-ordinator will speak to the FCG participants and explain the purpose of the FGC and their role, and will help them prepare for the meeting. The co-ordinator will agree on a neutral venue.

- **The meeting**

  The co-ordinator will chair the start of the meeting, inviting the child's social worker to open the meeting, outline the professionals' concerns and what would be an acceptable plan for the child. The process is important as family or friends may not be aware of the concerns or possible risks to the child, for example, if the mother has commenced a relationship with a man who is known to be a risk to children or, as in the Lesland case study, the mother is suffering from depression and that this is impacting on her care of the child.

It is helpful if the social worker prepares a written report that also includes any resources that are already being provided to the family, or what resources could be made available either by the local authority or by other services that the family could access. The report will also include any plan that may place the child at risk of harm and therefore would not be acceptable to the local authority. For example, in the Lesland case, Mrs Lesland's depression is placing the children at risk of neglect, and she requires support. Therefore, no support and leaving Mrs Lesland to continue as she is would not be an acceptable plan. This report can be left with the participants so that they can refer to it during the meeting. After the child's social worker's presentation, the social worker leaves the meeting, although they are available for any questions, and will rejoin the meeting after the participants have formulated a plan.

- **The plan**
  Thereafter, the FGC process operates with the assistance of the independent co-ordinator for the participants to formulate a plan or decision as to how to support the parents or meet the child's needs. To do this, the participants are advised by the co-ordinator of their tasks, which are to:

  - decide whether they agree or disagree with the professionals' concerns;

  - devise an agreed plan on how to meet the child's needs;

  - agree how the plan will be reviewed; and

  - agree on any contingency plans if the original plan does not work out.

- **Implementation and review**
  Once the co-ordinator has explained the tasks, the participants are given private time for how longer they require to formulate their plan. Once they are ready with a plan, the co-ordinator will return to the meeting to assist the family to formally record the plan, identifying any resources that may be needed, who will be responsible for the actions, and timescales. The child's social worker rejoins the meeting to discuss the plan. If the plan is acceptable to the child's social worker and does not place the child at risk of

harm, the social worker will take steps to implement it, such as commencing assessments of any family members who have decided to put themselves forward as alternative carers.

If there is a need to review the plan, timescales for this will be scheduled during the FGC, and the child's social worker will take the lead in organising this.

The Public Law Working Group (2019, para 90) found that FGCs are still not routinely offered across England and Wales prior to or subsequent to the pre-proceedings stage, and has recommended that they should be offered, prior to the child being taken into care, except in an emergency.

Flowchart 2: FGC process: Key stages

This flowchart details the key stages of the FGC process.

1 Referral

- Referrer/child's social worker decides on need for an FGC
- Parents' consents obtained
- Application form for an FGC is completed by social worker
- Case allocated to the Independent FGC Co-ordinator
- Extended family members identified
- Date and venue agreed for the FGC

2 Preparation

- FGC Co-ordinator engages directly with the child, parents, extended family and professionals in preparation of FGC

3 FGC meeting

Information sharing by referrer/child's social worker presenting:
- Introduction/explanation of process by the co-ordinator
- Co-ordinator agrees ground rules for the FGC meeting

- Introduction of participants
- Information given by the referrer/child's social worker includes:
    - Reasons/concerns held by referrer/child's services involvement,
    - What plan would not be acceptable to children's services
    - The issues to be addressed
    - Child's views and other key persons if unable to attend
    - Resources available from children's services

    This can be done in the form of a short report, which should be shared with participants before the FGC
- Participants/family members have an opportunity to ask the referrer/child's social worker questions or seek clarification
- Co-ordinator and referrer/child's social worker withdraw from the FGC

4 Private family time

Family members have four tasks:
- To decide whether they disagree with any concerns raised by the referrer/child's social worker
- Agree a plan
- Agree contingency plans
- Agree how to review plan

FGC co-ordinator is available to assist the family members

The plan will include:
- Who in the family will do what
- Who will check that actions agreed are undertaken
- Which professionals will have responsibility for ensuring the plan is implemented and for monitoring it
- Agreeing reviewing arrangements

5 Family plan presented, actions and contingency plan agreed

- Co-ordinator and referrer/child's social worker return
- Family members present the plan

- Negotiations undertaken to discuss help/resources
- Plan agreed with referrer/child's social worker, ensuring the child is not placed at risk of harm. If the plan does place the child at risk of harm, family members will be requested to reconsider the plan; if that is not agreed, the plan can be rejected by the referrer/child's social worker
- Contingency plan is considered
- Arrangements for review of the plan will be agreed

6   Implementation of the plan

- Family members are the guardian of the plan
- Family members and the child's social worker agree to ensure all agreed actions are fulfilled, and that all agree to work in partnership to take the plan forward within agreed timescales
- Family members appoint who in the family is responsible for reviewing the plan's progress
- Co-ordinator sends out copies of the plan to all family members

Another FGC can be requested if the plan needs changes, or to discuss progress/concerns

7   Review of the plan

- Plan reviewed with the family's agreement
- Support/resources and solutions sought for any actions not fulfilled

Flowchart 3: FCG process: Roles and responsibilities

This flowchart details the roles and responsibilities of the professionals and participants

Referrer/child's social worker

- To discuss with the family/those with parental responsibility the possibility of convening an FGC
- To meet the co-ordinator to discuss referral and convening of an FGC
- To explain the purpose of the FGC, to be clear about the non-negotiable position, that is, any conditions or limitations in the plan to ensure the child is not placed at risk of harm What if change does not occur, and timescales around this
- To provide clear, good quality information for the "information sharing" stage, being clear about care and protection issues for the child and potential availability of support/resources
- To be prepared to answer questions raised by family members to aid their understanding
- To liaise with the family monitor and be the "driver" of the plan
- To attend the FGC, and to be available for consultation, clarification and answer any questions the family have
- To agree the plan if it is safe to do so

The referal process

- The referrer/child's social worker must identify what their agency would consider unacceptable for the child
- The referral should include background information, the reason why children's services is involved and details of the family members to be invited to the FGC
- The FGC co-ordinator should be provided with some information explaining what decisions the referrer/child's social worker has made and could make in relation to the child, for example, commencement of legal proceedings

FGC co-ordinator's role

- To maintain an impartial and independent mediating role throughout the preparation, FGC process and meeting
- To meet with the referrer/child's social worker to discuss the referral
- To explore the wider family network
- To clarify the roles/responsibilities of all participants
- To identify if advocates are required
- To take the lead in preparing both family members and the referrer/child's social worker
- To be flexible and adaptable to the needs of each family member
- To visit each family member who is a potential participant to prepare them, wherever practically possible, and to ensure each is fully conversant with the FGC process and the issues that will be considered at the meeting
- To listen to all the viewpoints and assist to facilitate family members to ensure their voice is heard in a way that they want, even if they are unable to attend
- To identify if advocates, interpreters and other supporters are required to assist family members at the meeting
- To relay important queries and information between family members, with their permission, to enable the most effective meeting for everyone
- To organise practicalities of the FCG, such as venue and refreshments
- To chair the "Information Sharing" stage
- To be available, if necessary, to the family members throughout their "private family time"
- To help clarify the plan and its presentation to professionals
- To write up the plan and distribute it to all family members
- To check in with the child's social worker and family monitor to ensure the plan is working
- To arrange a review should family members or the child's social

worker consider this necessary
- To review any feedback received in relation to the process

FGC meeting: principles

- All have the right to clear and relevant information
- The meeting should be strengths-based and solution-focused
- The co-ordinator will ensure there are introductions, that the process is clarified and ground rules agreed

FGC process

The child's social worker will present information, to include:
- Current concerns and the reason for the FGC
- Details of the family's strengths and successes
- Clarity about what needs to change for the child and within what timescales
- Information about what resources could be available to support the family plan, any limitations on resources (including resources of time), timescales for accessing them, and any procedures to be followed to access resources
- Any child welfare concerns that will affect what can be agreed, such as the child not having contact with a particular person or the need for contact to be supervised;
- What action will be taken if family members are unable to formulate a plan, or the plan is not agreed, or if the concerns set out by children's services are not addressed in the plan. This could vary from "remaining concerned" to evoking statutory powers such as commencing legal proceedings

Family

- To decide whether they agree or disagree with any concerns raised by the referrer/child's social worker
- To devise and agree a plan to meet the child's needs
- To agree how this plan is to be reviewed
- To agree a contingency plan if the original is not working

Case study 6: An effective FGC

Karen has five children with three different fathers. All five children lived with Karen, a single parent who had successfully managed their care with the support of various paternal family members. Karen then met a new man, Fred. Within a short time, Karen and Fred decided to enter into a committed relationship and to live together, after Karen fell pregnant with her sixth child.

Fred was known to children's services as being a risk to children, having been convicted of inappropriate sexual activity with a minor, a 15-year-old girl who had been Fred's daughter's friend, who, with Fred's daughter and other minors, had attended Fred's home for a party. They had all drunk alcohol and Fred had admitted to having taken drugs. The 15-year-old minor made disclosures that Fred had attempted to engage in sexual activity with her. He was arrested, charged and pleaded guilty. One of the conditions placed on Fred as a result of his conviction was that he was not to have any unsupervised contact with any child, including his own daughter. This meant that any contact, even with his daughter, had to be supervised by a family member. Since his conviction, Fred's family members had supervised contact between Fred and his daughter. When Fred's daughter came to stay for overnight contact, Fred's brother or sister would stay over so that the contact was supervised at all times.

Karen, on finding herself pregnant, informed her extended family about Fred and his conviction, and the fact that she wanted to live with him. Karen's five children could not come with her, for two reasons:

● Firstly, due to Fred's conviction. All five children were minors; two were female and aged 12 and 14, similar ages to the minor with whom Fred had admitted to having inappropriate sexual conduct. Therefore, all contact between the five children and Fred would have to be supervised. Fred's family refused to assist with the supervision. Also, this level of supervision would place a heavy burden on Karen to ensure that she was always present, and practically this was not possible.

● Secondly, due to lack of accommodation. Fred lived in a two-bedroomed flat and therefore the children could not live with them there.

An FGC was convened and family members were called, including the three fathers of the five older children and members of the extended paternal family. The participants of the FGC were informed of the concerns relating to Karen's new partner and that the children could not live with Karen and Fred, and that any contact with Fred had to be supervised.

The fathers and members of the paternal family came forward and offered alternative long-term care for each of the five children. It was further agreed that Karen would have contact with the children in their new homes and that the children would not visit Karen or Fred in their home.

This was no doubt a difficult decision for Karen; however, the children were happy that, if they could not live with their mother, they would be living with their fathers and extended paternal family members, and were all physically close to each other.

The FGC process assisted in achieving a very effective outcome, as it meant that none of the five children had to be brought into local authority care and they remained cared for by either their birth fathers or paternal family members. No legal proceedings were commenced in relation to these children, as this was an agreed family arrangement. Unfortunately, this was not the case for the baby and, once born, care proceedings were issued due to the risk to the baby of sexual harm. Assessments were undertaken of the parents, including risk assessments. Fred and Karen were very co-operative and understood the reasons for the authority's concerns. Unfortunately for them, the relationship did not last and Karen moved out with the baby prior to the conclusion of care proceedings to live near her older five children. She already understood the concerns relating to Fred and agreed that any contact he had with the baby would be fully supervised by her. As a result, care proceedings were concluded with no order.

This was a good example of how FGCs can support families using the strengths-based approach, enabling them to take the lead in devising solutions, which they did. It empowered the family to implement the family plan, which they considered to be the one that best suited the children, rather than a plan being imposed on them by children's services. The case also demonstrates that for the five older children, the FGC process was critical in that it meant that they could remain in the care of their family, not requiring intervention by children's services and commencement of care proceedings.

---

10   The Lesland case: Part 7

The FGC is convened and Mr Lesland is contacted with a new mobile phone number provided by his mother. Mr Lesland confirms that he cannot attend as he is still living abroad and intends to remain there. Mrs Lesland's two siblings, Mrs Kalisha Petal and Ms Petra Price, attend, as does the paternal grandmother, Mrs Lesland senior.

The outcome of the FGC is that Mrs Petal offers to support Mrs Lesland by visiting the family home twice a week after school to help her prepare the evening meal. Ms Price is unable to offer support during the week as she lives over two hours drive away, but says that she can take care of Rachel and Josh over school holidays. Mrs Lesland senior states that she cannot offer support around long-term care of the children as she lives in a one-bedroomed flat and has health problems. She also wants contact with Caroline to be resumed.

The children's social worker re-devises a "child in need" plan, which includes additional support, as follows:

- the children's social worker is to make announced and unannounced visits to the family home;

- a family support worker will attend the home twice a week to help Mrs Lesland set morning routines to get the children to school/ nursery on time;

- funding will be provided for a twice weekly nursery placement for Caroline;

- breakfast and after school club will continue to be provided for Rachel and Josh on days when the family support worker is not attending the home;

- Mrs Lesland is to request her GP to make a referral for counselling.

Despite the "child in need" plan and the additional support, matters continue to deteriorate. Mrs Petal, Josh's teacher and the health visitor all report to the children's social worker that there has been no improvements. Mrs Petal is concerned that Rachel is undertaking a lot of Caroline's care as Mrs Lesland is still sleeping for many hours during the day.

The family support worker reports that, on three of her visits, Mrs Lesland did not open the front door, even though she was at home, and Caroline could be heard crying. The nursery is concerned about Caroline as she was observed with small bruises on her upper arms and has extensive nappy rash. Despite being advised, Mrs Lesland has not taken Caroline to see the GP or health visitor. The nursery teacher is of the view that the bruises appear to have been caused by rough handling. Mrs Lesland says that they were caused by Rachel picking Caroline up by her arms.

There are additional concerns raised by both the children's teachers and the nursery teacher that Mrs Lesland often smells of alcohol in the mornings. The children's social worker has not observed this on her visits but has noticed a number of wine bottles in the recycling bin. When asked, Mrs Lesland states that the neighbour keeps leaving her bottles there as her recycling bin is always full.

Despite several reminders from the children's social worker, Mrs Lesland has not made a GP appointment for the counselling referral. The social worker is concerned and, after speaking with her manager, it is agreed to escalate matters to child protection and to convene a child protection case conference.

---

11   Child protection case conferences

A child protection case conference is a meeting designed to enable the professionals involved in the child's life to assess all the relevant information and formulate a protection plan on how to safeguard the child and promote their welfare, whilst in the care of their parents. Its purpose is to make recommendations on how organisations and agencies will work together to safeguard the child in future (*Working Together*, HM Government, 2018, p 46). The parents and/or anyone significant to the child are invited to attend, together with the various professionals involved with the child, who may include the following:

- the child's social worker and/or any other staff members from children's services who have undertaken an assessment of the child and family;

- the foster carers (former or current if the child is in local authority care);

- health professionals involved in the child's life, such as a health visitor, school nurse, family doctor, or midwife (if the conference is a pre-birth conference dealing with the protection plan of the unborn);

- education professionals if the child is attending a school or nursery, such as the designated child protection officer from the school or nursery, class teacher, school nurse or head teacher;

- if the parents have involvement with other organisations such as adult mental health services, probation or drug and alcohol services, and professionals who know the parents from the relevant services;

- police and any other agencies such as the local housing authority that may have relevant information.

Any professional who has been invited but is unable to attend can send apologies and is requested to provide a report, or alternatively they can give verbal information to the child's social worker, which will be fed back at the conference.

It is important to know the child's views. Children can attend but if they do not, perhaps due to their young age, then their views and wishes will be included by the child's social worker in the report they present to the case conference.

Parents can attend with support either from a friend, advocate or their solicitor. Members of the extended family can also be invited.

The case conference is independently chaired. It will undertake the following:

- It will consider whether the child has suffered and/or is likely to suffer significant harm under any of the four categories of abuse (detailed below), as set out in *Working Together* (HM Government, 2018, p 100). If the professionals are in agreement that the child meets the criteria of significant harm, they will record it under the specific category/categories of abuse.

- It will consider and devise a protection plan to safeguard and promote the child's welfare. Actions will be listed for specific professionals and/or parents, together with timescales and alternative action if outcomes are not achieved.

- Finally, the independent Chair of the conference will summarise the main points and detail in the minutes the name of the allocated child's social worker. The Chair will also designate a core group of professionals and family members to implement the protection plan, including the child's social worker. The core group will meet or report to the child's social worker initially 10 days after the conference, and thereafter every 28 days, until the date of the review conference, in terms of the progress of the plan.

A review child protection case conference will be held within three months, or earlier if necessary, of the initial conference. Thereafter, subsequent review child protection case conferences are held every six months and can continue for however long the protection plan is necessary. However, in practice, if change has not occurred by the time of the second review, children's services should seek legal advice to consider what other options are available, such as convening an FGC or considering legal proceedings.

The purpose of review child protection case conferences is to monitor the effectiveness of the protection plan, whether the agreed action is being implemented, or whether the plan should be changed. If it is noted at the conference that there has not been any significant improvement, the Chair can include in the protection plan advice for the child's social worker to seek legal advice, if they have not already done so, to consider legal options available to further safeguard the child.

If care proceedings are commenced, then a review child protection case conference can decide that the protection plan is no longer necessary, given that the child has protection of the legal proceedings.

12   Categories of abuse

Abuse is defined by *Working Together* (HM Government, 2018, p 102) as a form of maltreatment of a child. Different types of abuse are formally grouped into four separate broad categories: physical abuse, emotional abuse, sexual abuse and neglect (pp 102–104). Children can be subject to one or more categories and can be recorded as having suffered actual abuse or to be at risk of it.

- Physical abuse involves hitting, shaking, throwing, poisoning, burning, scalding, drowning, suffocating, or otherwise causing physical harm to a child. It can also include when a parent or carer fabricates the symptoms of, or deliberately induces, illness in a child (p 102).

- Emotional abuse involves the persistent emotional maltreatment of a child so as to cause severe and persistent adverse effects to their emotional development. It can involve saying to them that they are worthless or unloved, inadequate, or valued only if they meet the needs of another (p 103).

  It can also include not giving a child opportunities to express their views, deliberately silencing them or "making fun" of what they say or how they communicate. It may feature age or developmentally inappropriate expectations being imposed on a child. It may include interactions that are beyond a child's developmental capability, as well as overprotection and limitation of exploration and learning, or preventing a child from participating in normal social interaction. It may involve a child seeing or hearing the ill-treatment of another, such as in domestic abuse. It may involve serious bullying, including cyber bullying, causing a child frequently to feel frightened or in danger, or the exploitation or corruption of a child (p 103).

  Some level of emotional abuse is involved in all types of maltreatment of children, although it may occur alone (p 103).

- Sexual abuse involves enticing or forcing a child to take part in sexual activities, not necessarily involving a high level of violence, whether or not the child is aware of what is happening. These activities may involve physical contact including assault by penetration (for example, rape or oral sex) or non-penetrative acts such as masturbation, kissing, rubbing and touching outside of clothing. They may also include non-contact activities, such as involving a child in looking at, or involvement in the production of, sexual images, watching sexual activities, encouraging a child to behave in a sexually inappropriate way, or grooming them in preparation for abuse. It can take place online, and technology can be used to facilitate offline abuse (p 103).

Sexual abuse can be perpetrated by males and females, adults and children, and both male and female children can be at risk (p 103).

Child sexual exploitation is a form of child sexual abuse.

● Neglect involves the persistent failure to meet a child's basic physical or psychological needs, likely to result in the serious impairment of their health or development. It may occur during pregnancy as a result of maternal substance abuse. Once a child is born, neglect may involve a parent or carer failing to:

a. *provide adequate food, clothing and shelter (including exclusion from home or abandonment);*

b. *protect a child from physical and emotional harm or danger;*

c. *ensure adequate supervision (including the use of inadequate caregivers);*

d. *ensure access to appropriate medical care or treatment.*

It may also include neglect of, or unresponsiveness to, a child's basic emotional needs (p 104).

---

13   The Lesland case: Part 8

At the initial child protection conference, all professionals were in agreement that Rachel and Josh have suffered significant harm, and all three children are at risk of suffering significant harm in the future. All three children are made subject to a protection plan under the category of Rachel and Josh having suffered neglect, and all three children being at risk of suffering neglect.

A protection plan is formulated. It states that if the mother's parenting and capacity to meet all three children's needs does not improve within three months, that is, by the review child protection case conference, the children's social worker should request a legal planning meeting to consider legal options available to the local authority in relation to safeguarding the children's welfare.

Flowchart 4: Child protection conference process

This flowchart details the child protection process.

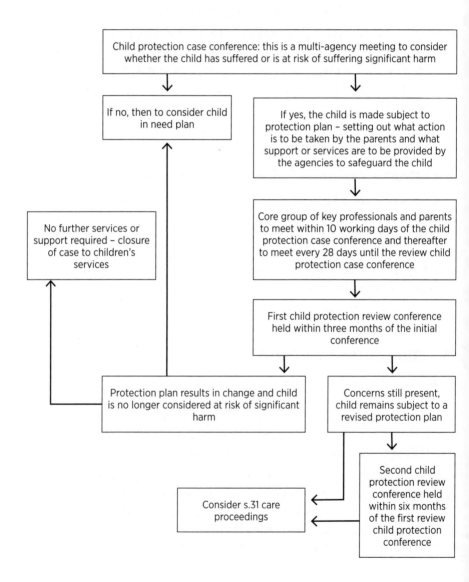

14 Criminal proceedings

It is important to note that if a child makes an allegation of child abuse or neglect, in addition to involvement of children's services, it can also result in commencement of a criminal investigation by the police. Police involvement can result in the commencement of a joint s.47 investigation with children's services. Police involvement does not prevent but can restrict children's services from undertaking its own enquiries. The child's social worker should always seek advice from the police investigating officer before asking any questions or taking any steps that could possibly jeopardise potential criminal investigation, as the threshold for criminal proceedings is higher than that for care or supervision order proceedings.

Should a child make an allegation of a child protection nature to anyone other than their social worker, such as their foster carer or a professional such as a school teacher or health professional, the procedure that should be followed is to record the exact words that the child states. Thereafter, the foster carer should contact their supervising social worker, or a professional should contact their manager or lead designated child protection officer in their service, for a referral to be made to a child's social worker or children's services. If in doubt, advice can be sought from the duty children's social worker from children's services.

Evidentially, following the correct procedure from the moment the allegation or disclosure is made is crucial in terms of attempting to secure a conviction in a criminal prosecution. As already mentioned, the threshold in criminal proceedings is much higher as the evidence has to prove the allegation beyond all reasonable doubt. This is different in care or supervision order proceedings, where the evidential threshold is to prove the evidence on a balance of probabilities.

15 The Lesland case: Part 9

Since the initial child protection conference, matters have deteriorated further.

On a home visit, the children's social worker found a man in the property who introduced himself as Mr Lee (aged 27). Mrs Lesland informed the social worker that Mr Lee was her boyfriend, and that although he was considerably younger than her, he was very mature and understanding. They had met via an internet dating site two weeks previously and instantly "clicked". Mrs Lesland explains to the social worker that she has informed Mr Lee in one of their phone conversations that she is finding it difficult to manage care of all the children, and that Mr Lee was so kind that he dropped everything and came to live with them to help her to care for the children.

The children's social worker asks for Mr Lee's consent to undertake police and local authority checks. Mr Lee consents and states that he had already explained his past to Mrs Lesland and had nothing to hide from her. Mrs Lesland informs the social worker that Mr Lee had told her that he had been to prison, but that it was not his fault, and that she did not care about his past as she could see that he was a generous, kind person and that is what is important for her. Mrs Lesland also informs the social worker that, since coming to the home, Mr Lee has decorated Rachel and Josh's bedroom at his own expense and that the children were so pleased that they had made him a thank you card. Mr Lee has even babysat Caroline, after he suggested Mrs Lesland go to bingo one evening a week.

The social worker expresses her concerns that Mrs Lesland had not informed her of the new relationship before Mr Lee moved in. She reminds Mrs Lesland that the children are subject to a child protection plan and that any significant changes that impact on them need to be discussed with her.

Mr Lee interrupts and states that Mrs Lesland has a right for her family life to be respected and does not need to tell the social worker about her personal life. The social worker reminds Mrs Lesland that her new relationship does affect the children.

With Mr Lee's consent, the children's social worker immediately requests police checks on Mr Lee, which reveal that he is considered to be a risk to children. He has a conviction for sexual intercourse with an underage female (aged 15), four years ago. The checks also reveal that a previous partner had alleged domestic abuse and that he had attempted to interfere inappropriately with the partner's four-year-old son. No charges had been brought regarding this allegation.

On receipt of this information, a s.47 investigation is commenced.

The Lesland case: Discussion

Mr Lee's conviction for an offence against a minor is very important as it provides clear evidence that a criminal court found beyond all reasonable doubt that he was found guilty of the offence. Unlike findings made in care proceedings, criminal convictions will follow the person; whenever Mr Lee enters a family where the children are known to children's services, information about his conviction will become available further to police checks and this, together with the information related to the previous partner, can be shared for child protection reasons.

In criminal proceedings, it is the Crown Prosecution Service (CPS, responsible for deciding whether to pursue the criminal prosecution) that decides whether there is sufficient evidence to commence a criminal prosecution. In the Lesland case, although allegations of sexual abuse were made regarding his previous partner's four-year-old child, the CPS may have decided not to pursue criminal proceedings as, due to the age of the child, it may have decided that it was unable to present sufficient evidence.

15.1   Multi-agency protection arrangements to manage risks

There are several additional processes to protect the public and those at particularly high risk of domestic abuse, from those classed as high risk violent or sexual offenders. These were established due to growing research recognising links between domestic abuse and child abuse (McKay, 1994).

15.2   Multi-Agency Public Protection Arrangements (MAPPA)

This is a process in which local police, prison and probation services, and other bodies dealing with offenders, work together to assess and manage the risks posed by violent or sexual offenders in the community. The agencies share information and devise plans to minimise risk by considering suitable accommodation, placing controls or intensive supervision on offenders, or requiring them to attend drug and alcohol programmes aimed at reducing further offending (National MAPPA Team, 2019).

Cases evaluated as high risk are referred to the Multi-Agency Risk Assessment Conference (MARAC). The MARAC co-ordinator will schedule a meeting in which information is shared between representative of local police, probation, health, children's services, housing services and the Independent Domestic Violence Advocate (IDVA), in relation to high risk domestic abuse cases. The forum also assesses victims' and their children's needs to consider options to manage or reduce risk. Agreed actions are carried out by individual agencies.

Domestic violence is defined as 'any incident of threatening behaviour, violence or abuse (psychological, physical, sexual, financial or emotional) between those aged 16 or over who are or have been intimate partners or family members regardless of gender or sexuality' (Home Office, 2013).

15.3   Multi-Agency Safeguarding Hub (MASH)

This is a single point of contact for safeguarding referrals, requesting advice or support for children and young people. Within the MASH, police, children's services, health and education services share information and work together to provide support at an early stage, to try to prevent children's needs increasing. Once a MASH referral is received, it is screened to consider the risk level and which team will deal with it. If the child already has an allocated social worker, the referral will be sent to them. If the MARAC process is triggered, it links with the MASH to safeguard the child.

16   Section 47: Duty to investigate

Section 47 of the Children Act 1989 places a statutory duty on the local authority to make enquiries, investigate, safeguard or promote the child's welfare, where it suspects that a child is suffering or likely to suffer significant harm.

> *(1) Where a local authority-*
>
> > *(a) are informed that a child who lives, or is found, in their area-*
> >
> > > *(i) is the subject of an emergency protection order; or*
> > >
> > > *(ii) is in police protection; or*

*(b) have reasonable cause to suspect that a child who lives, or is found,
in their area is suffering, or is likely to suffer, significant harm.*

If the decision is made that the criteria are met for consideration of a s.47
investigation, the process will begin with a strategy discussion, which is used to:

- share available information;

- agree action and timing of any criminal investigations;

- agree what information will be shared with the family;

- decide the initiation of a child and family assessment if one has not already
  been commenced or completed;

- agree a s.47 plan of enquiries to be undertaken and by which professional/s
  and when;

- agree what action or services are required to safeguard and promote the
  child's welfare;

- decide whether emergency or planned legal proceedings are to be
  commenced;

- decide whether a child protection case conference should be convened.

Section 47(5A) of the Children Act 1989 requires a local authority, where
practicable, to take account of children's wishes and feelings and give due
consideration (having regard to children's age and understanding) to such wishes
and feelings as ascertained, before determining what action to take during a s.47
investigation.

The outcome of the investigation will be recorded in writing and a copy given to
the parents and any professionals and agencies involved in the investigation.

Flowchart 1: *Initial referral* (in Chapter 5) shows how a referral could result
in a strategy discussion. Following from that stage, *Working Together* (HM
Government, 2018, p 41) provides a helpful flowchart of actions taken following a
strategy discussion (see Appendix 2).

17   The Lesland case: Part 10

The social worker asks Mr Lee to attend the local authority office, further to receipt of the information from the police of Mr Lee's conviction, and of the information relating to the allegations made by his ex-partner. Mr Lee explains to the children's social worker that he was wrongly convicted as the 15-year-old girl had told him that she was aged 18. In relation to the allegations by the ex-partner, he claims that these were maliciously made as the ex-partner would not accept that their relationship had come to an end and wanted to take revenge by making false allegations.

Mr Lee's consent is obtained to share the police information with Mrs Lesland.

The children's social worker informs Mrs Lesland, in Mr Lee's presence, of the information received from the police. Mrs Lesland informs the social worker that Mr Lee has explained everything and that she does not believe he presents a risk to her children.

The social worker explains that Mr Lee cannot live in the same household as the children. If Mrs Lesland does not agree to this, the local authority could provide the children with voluntary accommodation under s.20 of the Children Act 1989, to be placed in local authority foster care, with Mrs Lesland's consent, whilst the assessment of Mr Lee is undertaken. It is noted that at present no relative has been identified who could care for the children. If Mrs Lesland does not agree to this, then children's services would consider the immediate legal options available, including seeking an order to remove the children from her care until further assessments are completed.

Mrs Lesland asks the social worker whether, given that the conviction related to a 15-year-old girl, only Rachel could be accommodated as the other children are not at risk. The social worker explains that, in her view, given the information on Mr Lee, all the children are presently at risk. Mrs Lesland states that she does not want to ask Mr Lee to leave her home as she has felt so much better since he has been part of her life. She admits that she is unable to cope with the care of the children on her own and consents for all three children to be voluntarily accommodated, requesting that, if possible, they all be placed in the same foster placement. The social worker agrees to try her best for the children to be placed together; however, the placement will be dependent on what is available.

The fostering placement team cannot find a carer who is available to care for all three children. A decision is made for the children to be placed in two different placements: Rachel and Josh are placed together, and Caroline in a separate placement. Mrs Lesland is informed of this.

---

18 Section 20: Voluntary accommodation

As already discussed, local authorities have a duty to safeguard and promote the welfare of children within their area who are in need, which can be done by the provision of a range and level of services appropriate to those children's needs. One way in which a local authority can support children and families is by providing accommodation for a child in need in their area who may require it under s.20 of the Children Act 1989:

S.20 Children Act 1989 Provision of accommodation for children:

(1) Every local authority shall provide accommodation for any child in need within their area who appears to them to require accommodation as a result of—

(a) there being no person who has parental responsibility for him;

(b) his being lost or having been abandoned; or

(c) the person who has been caring for him being prevented (whether or not permanently, and for whatever reason) from providing him with suitable accommodation or care.

A child will only be eligible for accommodation if they fall within one of the criteria set out in s.20 of the Children Act 1989, which are that:

● There is no one with parental responsibility for them (s.20(1)(a)). Examples of children accommodated under this section could be orphaned children, or unaccompanied asylum-seeking children.

- The child is lost or has been abandoned (s.20(1)(b)).

- The person who has been caring for the child is prevented (whether or not permanently or for whatever reason) from providing the child with suitable accommodation and care (s.20(1)(c)). Under this provision, the local authority can provide accommodation even if a person who has parental responsibility is able to provide the child with accommodation, if the local authority considers that to do so would safeguard or promote the child's welfare (s.20(4)). The majority of children being provided with accommodation by the local authority fall under this category.

- The child has reached the age of 16 and the local authority considers that their welfare is likely to be seriously prejudiced if it does not provide them with accommodation (s.20(3)).

If it appears to the local authority that a child requires accommodation under s.20(1)(a), (b) or (c), this places on the local authority a statutory duty to place the child in local authority accommodation (this can be, for example, a foster placement, children's home placement, or with kinship/connected carers).

The local authority can only accommodate children aged under 16 under s.20 if all those with parental responsibility provide informed consent. If there is conflict between the parents/carers with parental responsibility, or if a parent objects and is able to provide or arrange accommodation then the local authority is unable to accommodate the child voluntarily (s.20(7) Children Act 1989).

Once a child is accommodated for more than 24 hours, their status becomes that of a child who is looked after, formerly called a "looked after child"; however, the local authority does not acquire parental responsibility and this remains solely with the parents. This is because s.20 of the Children Act is based on co-operative working between the local authority, the child and their parents. The authority to place a child in voluntary accommodation is not from a court order but from the parents who have parental responsibility providing voluntary consent.

As the accommodation is voluntary, the parents/carers with parental responsibility do not have to provide any form of notice if they wish to withdraw consent, which they can do at any time, and remove the child from voluntary accommodation (s.20(8)). The local authority cannot oppose the parent's request to end the s.20 voluntary arrangement. However, it is always advisable for a child's removal to be undertaken in a planned manner with agreement of the parents/carers so it is least disruptive to the child.

If the local authority takes the view that removal of the child from local authority accommodation will place the child at risk of significant harm, it will have to consider legal proceedings by seeking either an emergency protection order or interim care order to prevent the child's removal from local authority accommodation. The granting of either of these orders grants parental responsibility to the local authority for the duration of the order, enabling the authority to share parental responsibility with the parents. The authority can then ensure that the child is not removed from accomodation.

18.1 Benefits of section 20

Understandably, consenting to local authority accommodation is a very difficult decision for parents or carers to make and can raise negative feelings for the child/ren and parents. It will also be disruptive for the child, having them leave their home and requiring them to form relationships with carers if they are placed in foster care, or if they do not have a prior relationship with kinship carers.

However, s.20 voluntary accommodation can at times be an extremely effective and postive short-term provision of support. If properly used, s.20 can be a powerful tool, as it can provide an immediate solution perhaps when a family is in crisis, for example, if a parent or carer is prevented from caring for the child by being detained in hospital or prison for a short period of time and if there is no one else who can care for the child. Alternatively, a parent may acknowledge that they are currently unable to manage the care or parenting of their child and need support to do so, whether this is on a temporary or possibly permanent basis if there are no alternative family carers. Therefore in these situations, consenting to s.20 can be offered to support parents in times of difficulty.

This can be a positive way for authorities to provide accommodation for:

* children who have arrived in the UK as unaccompanied asylum-seeking

children, who do not have anyone to care for them;

- older children whose relationship with their parents or carers has presently broken down;

- if parents are unable to identify alternative carers, or the alternative carers are to be assessed;

- babies or young children, whose parent/s relinquish their child, who is then placed for adoption.

18.2 Proper use of section 20

If a parent or young person requests s.20 voluntary accommodation, the local authority will first endeavour to explore all other options, including other support or services for the child and/or family. The local authority's primary focus will be to keep the child in their home, and if necessary, the local authority will assess whether support or services are required to achieve this. If this is not possible, it will consider placement with extended family or people connected to the child. If an FGC has been undertaken, this may already have assisted in early identification of possible carers.

The process is initiated by the local authority commencing an assessment to consider:

- the child's needs;

- whether the child requires local authority accommodation; and

- the capacity of their parents/carers to respond appropriately to these needs.

  Before making any decision with respect to a child whom the local authority is looking after, or proposing to look after, it shall, so far as is reasonably practicable, ascertain the child's wishes and feelings.[104]

Due to the recognition of the evolving rights of a young person, should a young person aged 16 or 17 request accommodation, they do not need the consent

104 s.22(4) Children Act 1989

of those with parental responsibility in order to be accommodated by the local authority. Section 20(11) of the Children Act 1989 provides that if a child who has reached the age of 16 agrees to being provided with local authority accommodation, a person with parental responsibility for that child cannot remove them nor can they object to their being accommodated.

18.3 Contact

Once a child is placed under s.20 and accommodated away from their parents' care, the local authority should promote contact between the child, their parents and anyone else who is significant to the child. This is a statutory duty (Schedule 2 para 15(1) Children Act 1989).

18.4 Consequences of delay in care planning

In recent years, there has been a steady increase in the number of children voluntarily accommodated under s.20. As already stated, once accommodated, a child's status becomes that of a "looked after child", and therefore the local authority must formulate a care plan.

However, for the majority of children, s.20 should not be a long-term provision; therefore, if a child cannot be returned to their parent's or carer's care, the local authority should progress the child's permanency care plan by commencing proceedings without delay.

Increasing use of s.20 arrangements has resulted in local authorities facing a heightened level of judicial scrutiny and criticism of its inappropriate use and of what has been termed the "misuse" of s.20. Much of the judicial criticism has related to the poor practice of drift, with children spending lengthy periods of time accommodated under s.20 with no clear permanency plans and no plan to commence proceedings.

The former President of the Family Division, Sir James Munby, was particularly critical in the case of Re N.[105] In this case, the child had been placed under s.20

105 Re N (Children) (Adoption: Jurisdiction) [2015] EWCA Civ 1112

in May 2013, and care proceedings were not commenced until January 2014. His view was that allowing children to remain in s.20 with no proper plan to commence proceedings without delay was not just poor practice but wrong, as it denied both the parents and child the opportunity to be represented in court:

> *...misuse and abuse of section 20...is not just a matter of bad practice. It is wrong; it is a denial of the fundamental rights of both the parent and the child; it will no longer be tolerated; and it must stop.*[106]

In the case of *Worcestershire County Council v AA*,[107] the local authority faced judicial criticism for allowing AA, an accommodated child, to be 'left adrift in the care system'.[108] AA was accommodated in foster carer at the age of five (in 2010), due to concerns of physical abuse, emotional abuse and neglect. AA's mother died in 2017 and the father's identity was not known. The local authority did not issue care proceedings until 2018, when AA was aged 13, some eight years after first coming into local authority care.

The Judge noted that during this time AA had had 22 different social workers, and there had not been any consistent planning for AA. The local authority and the IRO service acknowledged that there had been a lack of effective care planning. The Judge concluded that the local authority had serially and seriously failed to meet AA's needs over a very prolonged period of time (para 68). Fortunately, AA had been provided with excellent care by his foster carers who, at the end of the proceedings, were granted a special guardianship order.

It is important for local authorities not to delay in the commencement of proceedings, for a number of reasons:

- Legal aid is not available automatically to a parent with parental responsibility, when their child is accommodated under s.20, if the local authority has not commenced the process of considering legal proceedings. Conversely, immediately on the notification of proposed care proceedings, parents with parental responsibility will be entitled to limited legal aid (Legal Help). On

---

106 *Re N (Children) (Adoption: Jurisdiction)* [2015] EWCA Civ 1112
107 *Worcestershire County Council v AA* [2019] EWHC 1855 (Fam)
108 Para 72

the commencement of care or supervision order proceedings, a parent with parental responsibility will automatically be eligible for the full legal aid entitlement.

- Children do not have independent representation whilst accommodated in local authority care under s.20 and their views are heard through the social worker and their IRO. Children who are accommodated under s.20, as they aquire a looked after status, are entitled to the appointment of an IRO, who is responsible for reviewing the child's care plans. However, the child will only be eligible for independent representation on the commencement of care or supervision order proceedings. Once proceedings are initiated, this automatically entitles the child to the benefit of independent representation through the appointment of a Children's Guardian from CAFCASS and legal representation from their children's solicitor, who will both represent their views and safeguard their interests independently of children's services.

- Once care or supervision order proceedings are commenced, the case comes under the scrutiny of the court, and is subject to the statutory timescales as set out in the Public Law Outline (PLO). When children are in s.20 accommodation, there are no statutory timescales, and no judicial oversight or scrutiny of their placement or care plan. By not issuing proceedings, the court also has no ability to prevent or reduce unnecessary delay.

- Section 20 accommodation is not appropriate where there is an issue about a parent's mental capacity (other than for a short period before the commencement of care or supervision order proceedings) as questions can arise as to their ability to give informed consent to s.20.

- Section 20 accommodation is not appropriate where there are significant factual issues that need to be determined by the court before a final welfare decision can be made (other than for a short period before issuing care proceedings), for example, where a child has suffered a serious injury and no plausible explanation has been offered by the parents.

- Local authorities need to be very careful not to put parents under duress to agree to s.20 accommodation, as parents may themselves be vulnerable. There is inevitably an imbalance of power between the parents and local authority, as was recognised by the Supreme Court in the case of *Williams and Another v LB Hackney*[109] (see below).

- Local authorities should not use s.20 accommodation to avoid the more stringent legal test required by the court in the commencement of an application for an emergency protection order under s.44 of the Children Act 1989, or an interim care order under s.38 of the Children Act 1989.

- Section 20 requires working in partnership with the child's parents. It is not appropriate where it is no longer possible to do so.

In *Re N (Children) (Adoption: Jurisdiction)*,[110] Sir James Munby further highlighted why the proper use of s.20 is necessary due to its impact on:

- the failure of obtaining "genuine consent" from those who have parental responsibility

- the risk that children in s.20 arrangements are left there too long. It was acknowledged that s.20 did have a proper role to play as a short-term measure pending the commencement of care proceedings; however, to use it as a prelude to care proceedings for a lengthy period of time was 'wholly unacceptable' and 'a misuse of the local authority's statutory powers';[111]

- local authorities' attempts to impose on parents conditions to give seven days' notice of their intended withdrawal of consent which is not supported by the law. Sir James Munby made it clear that such practice must stop.

As a result of local authorities' poor practice, the court will be alert and the local authority can be subjected to probing questions to determine whether it has misused its powers. If this is found to be the case by the court, it could result in possible exposure to human rights claims. Sir James Munby, in *Re N*,[112] suggested good practice guidance for local authorities to follow when entering into s.20 arrangements, as follows:

109 *Williams and Another v LB Hackney* [2018] UKSC 37
110 *Re N (Children) (Adoption: Jurisdiction)* [2016] 1 FLR 621, CA
111 *Re N (Children) (Adoption: Jurisdiction)* [2015] EWCA Civ 1112, para 157
112 *Re N (Children) (Adoption: Jurisdiction)* [2015] EWCA Civ 1112

- Where possible, the agreement of a parent to a s.20 arrangement should be properly recorded in writing and evidenced by the parent's signature.

- The written document should be clear and precise and drafted in simple and straightforward language that the parent can readily understand.

- The written document should clearly state that the parent can "remove the child" from local authority accommodation "at any time".

- The written document should not seek to impose any limitations on the parent's right to withdraw consent.

- Where the parent is not fluent in English, the written document should be translated into the parent's own language and the parent should sign the foreign language text, adding, in the parent's language, words to the effect that 'I have read this document and I agree to its terms'.

Re N is an important case as it clarifies that failure to comply with obtaining valid consent could result in serious consequences for the local authority, such as exposure to claims for damages for non-compliance.

However, in the later case of *Williams and Another v LB Hackney*,[113] it was clarified that the guidance set out in Re N was only suggested guidance and does not impose any formal requirements in relation to the consent that is needed. However, it may assist if children's social workers considered addressing the matters listed as good practice detailed in the suggested guidance with parents when s.20 consent is being requested.

Williams and Another v LB Hackney[114] is another helpful case on the issue of s.20 where the Supreme Court provided guidance on its application. The parents had eight children, ranging in age from eight months to 14 years. One of the children (aged 12) was caught shoplifting chocolate bars and was arrested. He informed the police that the bruise on his face was caused by his father, who had beaten him with a belt. The police visited the family home and found it to be in a poor and unhygienic state. There was no food in the fridge and the children

113 *Williams and Another v LB Hackney* [2018] UKSC 37
114 *Williams and Another v LB Hackney* [2018] UKSC 37

appeared unkempt and dirty. Bound sticks were found in the home, suggesting that they may have been used to apply or threaten corporal punishment. The police decided that the children could not remain in the home, as it was unfit for habitation. The police exercised their powers of protection under s.46 of the Children Act 1989 and removed all eight children from the parents' care.

The parents were made the subject of police bail conditions prohibiting them from having any unsupervised contact with the children in order to prevent interference with them.

The next day, the parents were asked by children's services to sign a s.20 agreement, which was termed a "safeguarding agreement", requesting the parents' consent for the children to remain in foster care. The parents were not informed that they had the right (under s.20(8) of the Children Act 1989) to remove their children from local authority accommodation at any time. Both parents signed the agreement. A few days after giving consent, the father gave notice to withdraw his consent. Children's services were in agreement that the children could return home safely; however, they could not return them until the police bail conditions were varied, which was some two months later.

The parents commenced legal proceedings against the local authority, arguing that its actions were not in compliance with s.20 and were in breach of their Article 8 ECHR rights, in that the parents' consent had been unfairly obtained and therefore had not been true consent, and so the children had been unlawfully accommodated. Although at first hearing the parents were successful, on appeal, this decision was overturned. It was ruled that, in the absence of an unequivocal objection during the children's period of accommodation, the local authority had lawfully accommodated them under s.20.

Lady Hale gave the leading judgement in the Supreme Court and took the view that it was more helpful to focus on whether a parent has delegated their parental responsibility to the local authority in a way that is "real and voluntary" or "truly voluntary", rather than whether the child has been provided with accommodation by the local authority under s.20 of the Children Act 1989. Parents have a right to object, as s.20 does not give the local authority compulsory powers over the parents or child and must not be used in such a way as to give the impression that it does.

18.5 Valid section 20 consent

To understand the local authority's responsibility in acquiring valid consent to s.20, it will be of assistance to social workers to consider the helpful guidance provided in *Coventry City Council v C, B, CA and CH*.[115]

A mother with learning difficulties gave birth to her child after a caesarean section. Immediately after giving birth, she was requested by the local authority to agree to s.20 voluntary accommodation. She had already had three previous children removed, who were subject to placement orders, giving the local authority permission to place them for adoption. The mother initially refused to consent to the s.20 agreement; however, when she was approached again, after receiving post-operative morphine medication, she consented.

The Judge in this case set down useful guidance for social workers to follow when seeking s.20 voluntary consent from a parent, summarised as follows:

- Every social worker obtaining such a consent is under a personal duty to be satisfied that the person giving consent does not lack the capacity to do so.

- If the social worker has doubts about the parent's capacity, no further attempt should be made to obtain consent on that occasion and advice should be sought from the social work team manager or senior management.

- If the social worker is satisfied that the person whose consent is sought does have capacity, the social worker must be satisfied that the consent is fully informed and be satisfied by the following questions:

  (a) Does the parent fully understand the consequences of giving such a consent?

  (b) Does the parent fully appreciate the range of choices available? The parent should not feel that they have no choice. Equally, has the parent been

115 *Coventry City Council v C, B, CA and CH* [2012] EWHC 2190 (Fam)

informed of the consequences of refusing? That is, the local authority has the power and duty to commence care proceedings, if there are reasonable grounds to believe that the child is at risk of significant harm. It is advisable to ensure that the parent fully understands the authority's proposed plan, and the parent should be advised to seek independent legal advice.

(c) Is the parent in possession of all the facts and issues material to the giving of consent?

- If the social worker is satisfied that the consent is fully informed, then it is necessary to be further satisfied that the giving of such consent and the subsequent removal is both fair and proportionate, and the social worker may need to consider:

(a) What is the current physical and psychological state of the parent?

(b) Has the parent instructed a solicitor, or have they been encouraged and supported to seek legal advice prior to giving consent?

(c) Is it necessary for the safety of the child for them to be removed at this time? Are there any other options, for example, to remain in the parent's care with protective measures to safeguard the child whilst assessments are undertaken?

(d) Would it be fairer in this case for this matter to be the subject of a court order rather than a s.20 agreement?

In summary, to ensure that valid consent has been provided for s.20 voluntary accommodation, the social worker should make the following enquiries:

- Who has parental responsibility and how was it acquired?

- Do those with parental responsibility clearly understand what they are consenting to?

- Have they signed the s.20 accommodation agreement freely, understanding that they can withdraw their consent at any time?

- Finally, in light of the Coventry case, the Judge advised that local authorities may want to approach with great care the obtaining of s.20 agreements from mothers in the aftermath of birth, especially where there is no immediate danger to the child and where probably no order would be made.

A helpful template for a s.20 agreement has been provided by the Public Law Working Group (2019, pp 248–252), reproduced in Appendix 3.

18.6 Section 20 and human rights issues

There are two issues that local authorities must be alert to: misuse of s.20, and delay in making decisions about a child's future. If either of these issues are raised once court proceedings are commenced, the authority could face a human rights claim that, if successful, could result in the authority being ordered to pay damages for breaches of the child's or parents' rights.

The local authority must work in partnership with parents and should not use the threat of direct or indirect police involvement as a way to coerce parents to consent to s.20. Such action would be viewed as inappropriate and possibly an unlawful way to obtain parents' s.20 consent and will be open to human rights challenges, as clearly stated by the Judge in *Surrey County Council v M, F & E*:[116]

> To use the section 20 procedure in circumstances where there was the overt threat of a police protection if they did not agree, reinforced by the physical presence of uniformed police officers, was wholly inappropriate. By adopting this procedure, the local authority sought to circumvent the test any court would have required them to meet if they sought to secure an order, either by way of an emergency protection order or interim care order.

Case study 7: Obtaining consent

Syla, aged seven, disclosed to his class teacher at school that his mother had smacked him. He showed where he had been smacked, and the teacher could see visible bruising on the child's upper arms. An immediate referral was made

116 *Surrey County Council v M, F & E* [2012] EWHC 2400, para 60

to children's services. The local authority commenced a s.47[117] child protection investigation jointly with the police. As mentioned previously, a s.47 investigation is instigated if children's services is concerned that there is reasonable cause to suspect that the child is suffering or likely to suffer significant harm.[118]

The child was medically examined and the injuries to his arms were found to be non-accidental and consistent with the allegations made by Syla.

The mother, a single parent, had no family in this country. Her first language was not English; although she could understand it, she preferred to use an interpreter.

The mother was arrested and taken to the police station. The social worker asked, through a telephone interpretation service, whether, whilst investigations were being undertaken, the mother would agree for the child to be accommodated in foster care under s.20 of the Children Act 1989.

The mother was understandably upset. She denied hitting Syla and refused to provide her consent for s.20. The police officer intervened and stated to the mother that if she did not agree, Syla would still be put in care and that she would find it difficult to see him, and so it was better for her to agree now.

After the officer finished speaking, the social worker correctly explained that if she did not agree, due to the high level of concerns, emergency legal steps could be taken to enable the local authority to place Syla in foster care, but that even if those steps were taken, she would still be able to have contact with him. The social worker further explained to the mother that she could be assisted by being provided with a list of local children solicitors who could advise her of the available legal options.

The mother contacted a solicitor and arrangements were made for the mother to speak to the solicitor. The mother confirmed through the telephone interpretation service to her solicitor that she understood what the social worker had said. The mother thereafter confirmed to her solicitor her consent for Syla to be placed in foster care for a few days until the local authority commenced care proceedings. The social worker explained to the mother that, at court, the local authority would

117 Children Act 1989
118 S.47(1)(b) Children Act 1989

136

be seeking an interim care order in respect of Syla and for the court's permission that he remain in foster care pending further assessments.

At the first hearing, the mother's solicitor raised the issue as to whether valid consent for s.20 had been obtained, given what the police had said to the mother at the police station. The court directed the social worker who had been present at the police station to provide a statement to the court explaining the circumstances prior to the mother giving her s.20 consent. The social worker detailed in her statement what had occurred. On receipt of the statement, the court and the other parties did not raise any further objections and accepted that valid consent had been provided by the mother.

18.7 Impact of delay

Section 20 of the Children Act 1989 imposes no limit on the duration of accommodation. However, the local authority's general duties towards a looked after child, such as the duty to safeguard and promote a child's welfare, need to be taken into account in deciding for how long a child is to be accommodated under s.20.

As already discussed, once s.20 consent is received, the local authority must not delay in the implementation of the child's care plan without justification, otherwise it can face the court's scrutiny of the delay that has been caused and the impact on the child.

In a landmark case of *Northamptonshire County Council v AS and Others*,[119] the local authority was heavily criticised due to the inappropriate use of s.20 and the lack of progress of the child's case. The child, DS, was voluntarily accommodated under s.20 at 15 days old; the mother's wish was for the child to be adopted. The local authority failed to take any legal action until the child was some nine months old, at which time care proceedings were finally commenced.

---

119 *Northamptonshire County Council v AS and Others* [2015] EWHC 199

The Judge was of the view that no satisfactory explanation was provided for these extraordinary delays. The Judge explained that the practical effect of s.20 was that it deprived DS of the benefit of having a Children's Guardian to represent and safeguard his interests. It also deprived the court of the ability to manage the planning for DS and to prevent or reduce unnecessary and avoidable delay in securing a permanent placement for him at the earliest possible time. The Judge ordered the local authority to pay £17,000 for damages for breaches of human rights following a "truly lamentable" (as described by the Judge) catalogue of errors, omissions, delays and serial breaches of court orders in a child care case. This case demonstrates the importance of not allowing a case to drift, and that delay can be extremely damaging, not only to the local authority's purse but, more importantly, due to breaches of the children and family's human rights. The delay in this case could have been prevented by formulating a clear care plan that was required given that DS was a child who was looked after, and which was regularly reviewed. By doing this, it would have enabled progress of the case to be carefully monitored.

This case is considered to be a landmark, in that it was the first case where a local authority was ordered to pay damages for human rights failings in care proceedings. It has been followed by numerous others.

In the case of *Kent County Council v M and K (s.20 Declaration and Damages)*,[120] a human rights claim was brought against the local authority for a declaration that it had breached the child, K's, Article 6 and 8 ECHR rights and damages were sought. K had been accommodated under s.20. The claim was that there had been no assessments, too many foster placements, and that the local authority had been too slow to commence care proceedings. The court found that the local authority had breached both articles in that it had failed to:

- properly assess K for a period in excess of three years;

- implement a care plan that met K's needs for a period in excess of three years.

Resulting in:

- failure to provide K with a proper opportunity to secure a long-term

120 *Kent County Council v M and K* (s.20 Declaration and Damages) [2016] EWFC 28

placement and have a settled home life (breach of Article 8 ECHR); and

- failure to commence proceedings in a timely manner, depriving K of the protection as provided under the Children Act 1989, that is, access to court and procedural protection of a Children's Guardian (breach of Article 6 and 8 ECHR).

In summary

- Section 20 of the Children Act 1989 remains a useful and entirely appropriate tool for providing stable placements for children whose parents (for whatever reasons) are not able to offer them suitable accommodation and who are in agreement with the local authority's plan.

- There is no statutory time period as to how long children can remain in s.20 accommodation. It depends on the circumstances of the case and the child's care plan. If the local authority is considering issuing proceedings, then s.20 accommodation should only be for a short period unless there is a clear care plan that is fully agreed with the parents.

- Parents can withdraw consent at any time. It is therefore important for the children's social work team to develop an effective working relationship with the parents, supporting them to recognise and understand the child's needs.

- Section 20 remains an effective short-term solution to urgent child protection concerns, with parents providing consent to s.20 accommodation until the local authority issues its application in the Family Court.

- Section 20 remains an effective longer term solution for certain categories of children. This was recognised by Lady Hale in *Williams and Another v LB Hackney*.[121] Examples given were as follows:

  - disabled children where parents are entirely in agreement with the local authority's plan;

  - unaccompanied asylum-seeking children.

121 *Williams and Another v LB Hackney* [2018] UKSC 37

- Local authorities must ensure that children and families are treated fairly and that informed consent is obtained.

- To avoid drift and delay, children's services must ensure that there is a clear and effective care plan that is being implemented, is subject to regular reviews and updated, further to assessments of the child's changing needs or the parents' changing circumstances.

18.8 Support for accommodation for 16- and 17-year-olds

The local authority's responsibility for accommodating homeless 16- and 17-year-olds was widened by the case of *R (G) v Southwark LBC*.[122] This was a landmark judgement and, despite its age, is still a very relevant and important ruling in relation to accommodation for 16- and 17-year-olds. As a result of this case's impact, the Government provided guidance (Ministry for Housing, Communities and Local Government and DfE, 2018). In this case, G had been excluded from his home due to a family breakdown, and as a result was "sofa surfing", sleeping on friend's sofas and in cars. Aged 17, G requested children's services to provide him with accommodation as he was homeless. Children's services took the view that it would assist G under s.17 as a child in need by making a referral to the housing department for accommodation, but would not provide services under s.20.

G challenged this decision on the basis that he met the criteria as set out in s.20 and therefore should be provided with accommodation under it, as that would also provide the benefit of additional support from the local authority under the duties set out in the Children (Leaving Care) Act 2000 when he turned 18.

The local authority in the court proceedings responded that it should be permitted to consider all other sources of accommodation available to the child. Therefore, if appropriate accommodation was available, under s.17 of the Children Act 1989 the authority would not need to exercise its duties under s.20. This was rejected by the law lords and it was held that s.20 takes precedence; and therefore, if a child requires accommodation, this must be provided by children's

---

122 *R (G) v Southwark LBC* [2009] UKHL 26

services under s.20 of the Children Act 1989 and not under s.17 of the Children Act 1989.

To assist the local authority in deciding on the support to be provided, the leading Judge in *G v Southwark* relied on the list of questions set out in the earlier case of *R (A) v LB Croydon*,[123] as set out below and considered in an assessment:

1. **The child must be a child.** If this is not confirmed or there is doubt, then the local authority will have to undertake an age assessment.

2. **The child must be within the local authority's area.** The duty can arise if the child is present and is not ordinarily resident in the area. However, costs can be recouped from the local authority where the child is found to be ordinarily resident, or that local authority can accept responsibility for the child's case.

3. **Is the child a child in need?** In the case of *G v Southwark*, the law lords stated that this required "careful assessment".

4. **The child must require accommodation.** In the assessment, have all available options been considered, for example, the child may not be able to live with their parents but they could go and live with a relative and require support to get there, which could be provided under s.17.

5. **The child's need for accommodation must fall within the criteria as set out in s.20 of the Children Act 1989.** The majority of children will fall under the criteria that the carer is prevented from providing the child with suitable accommodation or care (s.20)(1)(c), as was the case in *G v Southwark*.

6. **What are the child's wishes and feelings?**

7. **What consideration has been given to those wishes and feelings?**

In the case of *Re G v Southwark*, the leading Judge also observed that s.27 of the Children Act 1989 did enable children's services to ask other authorities, including any local housing authority, for "help in the exercise of any of their functions" under Part III of the Children Act 1989; and that the requested authority must provide that help if it is compatible with their own statutory or other duties and

123 *R (On the Application of A) (FC) v LB Croydon* [2009] FCR 317, [2009] UKSC 8

did not unduly prejudice the discharge of any of their own functions. This does not mean that children's services can avoid their responsibility; rather, they can seek assistance from another authority to use its powers to help it discharge its own duties.

19   Unaccompanied asylum-seeking children

Children's services are responsible for the care of unaccompanied asylum-seeking children (UASC). These are children or young people under the age of 18, who have no parent or guardian in the UK to care for them, and who apply for asylum in the UK. Asylum can only be applied for once the child or young person is in the UK, and it can be applied for as early as at the point of first arrival in the UK, at the port of entry, for example, an airport. Once the application for asylum is made to an immigration officer, and the child or young person is accepted as being aged under 18, they will be granted the immigration status of "temporary admission". Thereafter, the young person will be granted "discretionary leave" for a limited period of time or until they reach 18. During this period, the young person cannot be removed from the UK until their asylum application has been determined,[124] which is usually after their 17th birthday.

Unaccompanied asylum-seeking children are placed in the care of the local authority and are looked after children.

Children who are accompanied by an adult are not required to seek asylum in their own right. The adult the child has accompanied can apply for asylum and the child will be treated as a dependent of the adult. Adults with children are supported by the National Asylum Support Scheme.

19.1   Age assessment

The decision about whether or not the UASC is presenting as a child can be difficult to ascertain, as the young person may not have any supporting documentation that establishes their age, nationality or identity. There may be many reasons for this, the child may have been trafficked with the use of false

124 Convention relating to the Status of Refugees 1951.

travel documents; they may have been advised to destroy their travel documents en route by their traffickers or agents so that it becomes more difficult to remove them from the country. Or they themselves, being an adult, may wish to present as a child due to the different level of support that is available, including that a child's asylum application will generally only be dealt with nearer to their 18th birthday and not before their 17th birthday.

In cases where the young person's given age is not accepted, it is the local authority's responsibility to ascertain it by conducting an age assessment. This is undertaken by two social workers from children's services. The social workers will ask the young person a series of questions, which will assist them to make a determination of the child's age. There is no statutory guidance on how to conduct an age assessment; however, the process that should be undertaken has been established in the case of R (On the Application of B) v London Borough of Merton.[125] Further guidance is provided by the ADCS (2015).

If the young person does not accept the outcome of an age assessment, they can either make a formal complaint or, more likely, threaten to challenge the assessment by making an application for judicial review. This is an application to a High Court Judge requesting that the Judge review the local authority's process in how the age assessment was conducted.

If the local authority is looking after the young person, then they should also support them to obtain independent legal advice in relation to their immigration matter and any age assessment dispute.

The landmark case known as the Hillingdon Judgement[126] established that, whilst the local authority is caring for a UASC who is under the age of 18, the young person will be accommodated under s.20 of the Children Act and considered to be looked after under s.22 of the Children Act.[127] As a result, UASC are therefore entitled to the same services under the Children Act as any child who is looked after by the local authority, including the provision of leaving care support depending on their eligibility category.

125 R (On the Application of B) v London Borough of Merton [2003] EWHC 1689 (Admin)
126 Behre & Ors, R v Hillingdon London Borough Council [2003] EWHC 2075 (Admin)(HC)
127 Behre & Ors, R v Hillingdon London Borough Council [2003] EWHC 2075 (Admin)(HC)

20 Child looked after

A child looked after (formerly known as a looked after child or a child in care) is a child who is in the care of the local authority for more than 24 hours.

Section 22 Children Act 1989 details:

(1) a child who is looked after by a local authority is a reference to a child who is—

(a) in their care; or

(b) provided with accommodation by the authority

There could be a variety of reasons why a child or young person may become looked after, such as:

- the child's parents agree to this by giving consent for the child to be accommodated in local authority care, under s.20 of the Children Act;

- the child is a UASC, with no responsible adult able to care for them;

- children's services has intervened because the child is at risk of significant harm and has been granted an emergency protection order under s.44 of the Children Act 1989, an interim care order under s.38, or a care order under s.31;

- a young person who is aged 16 or over requests to be accommodated, perhaps due to relationship difficulties with the parent;

- a child is involved in the criminal justice system and has been remanded to the care of the local authority due to a criminal offence.

Section 22 of the Children Act 1989 places a general duty on the local authority in relation to children who are looked after by the local authority. Section 1(1) of the Children and Social Work Act 2017 introduced corporate parenting principles that all local authorities must have regard to. These principles strengthen s.22 of the Children Act 1989 and the duties to children who are looked after, and require the local authority to do the following:

- to act in the child's best interests, promoting physical health, mental health and well-being;

- to encourage children to express their views, wishes and feelings and to take them into account;

- to promote children and young people to gain access to, and make best use of, the services of the local authority and partner services;

- to promote high aspirations and seek to secure best outcomes for children and young people;

- to provide children and young people with safety and stability in their home lives, relationships, education or work;

- to prepare children and young people for adulthood and independent living.[128]

Once looked after, the child will be allocated a social worker, who has a responsibility to visit the child within one week of the start of any placement, and then at intervals of no more than six weeks for the first year. Thereafter, if the placement is long term and designed to last until the child's 18th birthday, they must visit at intervals of no more than three months.[129]

A child is no longer a child looked after if:

- the child leaves care, is made the subject of a child arrangements order or a special guardianship order, or the care order is discharged;

- the child is made subject to an adoption order,

- the child is no longer being provided with accommodation under s.20 of the Children Act 1989 and returns home;

- the child turns 18 and is therefore no longer a child.

20.1 Drawing up a care plan

For a child of any age who is able to express their wishes and feelings and whom the local authority is proposing to look after or whom they are currently looking

128 s.1(1) Children and Social Work Act 2017
129 Care Planning, Placement and Case Review (England) Regulations 2010, regulation 28

after, the local authority will endeavor to ascertain the wishes and feelings of the child before making any decision and as is reasonably practicable.

Once the local authority decides that it would be in the child's best interests for accommodation to be provided, statutory guidance and regulations require a care plan to be drawn up in consultation with the child, their parents or carers, and the child's social worker.

If the accommodation of the child is a planned decision, then the child's care plan should be written before the child comes into care; however, if it is an emergency the care plan should be drafted as soon as possible.

Regulation 5(b) of the Care Planning, Placement and Case Review (England) Regulations 2010 specifies that the care plan should include how the local authority is to meet the child's needs in relation to their:

- plan for permanency;

- health, including a health plan;

- education and training, including, if relevant, a personal education plan;

- emotional and behavioral development;

- identity, religious persuasion, racial origin and cultural and linguistic background;

- family and social relationships;

- social presentation; and

- self-care skills.

Copies of the child's care plan are to be provided to the child (if they are of an age and understanding and if this does not place the child at risk of significant harm). Alternatively, an edited copy can be provided. Copies should also be provided to the parents, the IRO and the fostering service provider or care home (Regulation 6(4)).

The care plan will be reviewed at the child's looked after review.

20.2 Foster care

If the child is placed in foster care, they are considered as a child who is looked after within the meaning of s.22(1) of the Children Act 1989.

Foster carers are formally assessed and approved to care for children who are looked after. Approved kinship or connected carers are approved to care for a specific child who is looked after and who may also be related to them.

Foster carers are either approved by a local authority or independent fostering provider (IFP), and can be registered for:

- short-term foster placements: this can include caring for a child overnight or for longer periods. These placements are not considered the child's permanent placement;

- long-term or permanent foster placements: the child has been matched to this foster carer and they are considered the long-term carer who is providing a long-term home for the child;

- emergency foster care placements: this includes foster carers who offer emergency care for unplanned placements, perhaps during the evenings, weekends or holidays when children's services is closed;

- parent and child foster care placements: these placements provide support and guidance to parents before or after the birth of a child. The parent will live with their child in the foster placement until the conclusion of assessments as to the parent's capacity to care for the child;

- respite foster care placements: these are provided on a part-time basis, for a few hours, weekends, or while the child's family or foster carer take a holiday or break;

- remand foster care placements: this is an alternative to youth custody;

- kinship/connected carer placements: foster carers who are approved to care for a specific child.

20.3 Kinship care

If it is considered in a child's welfare that they cannot live with their parents, either temporarily or long term, then the local authority has a statutory duty under s.22C(6)(a) of the Children Act 1989 to seek a placement of the child with a relative, friend or connected person, unless such a placement does not meet the child's needs or is not consistent with their welfare. This principle was reinforced by the Public Law Outline (PLO), placing an expectation on local authorities to consider family members, friends and connected persons as either potential support to the parents in the child's care, or as possible short- or long-term carers. As discussed earlier, this process is greatly assisted by the early convening of an FGC or a similar model, such as a Family Network Meeting, so that those family or friends who are willing and able to assist are identified and assessed without delay. The local authority must first consider whether the child can be placed with any family members or friends, that is, a person connected to the child (connected person) who comes forward to be assessed.

20.4 Connected person

A connected person is defined by Regulation 24 of the Care Planning, Placement and Case Review (England) Regulations 2010 as being a relative, friend or other person connected with the child. *The Family and Friends Care Statutory Guidance for Local Authorities* (DfE, 2010, p 6, para 1.6) defines a connected person in the same terms. The guidance further states that a person connected with a looked after child may be someone who knows them in a more professional capacity, such as a child-minder, teacher or youth worker.

If such a person is identified, the local authority will undertake an assessment to consider their suitability to meet the child's needs. The assessment of kinship carers is a two-stage process. Firstly, a viability assessment is undertaken, which can take up to a maximum of two–three weeks. If the assessment is positive, then the child can be placed with these carers. Once placed, the child is a looked after child and the carer is entitled to all the support of a foster carer. This includes the fostering allowance and the support of a supervising social worker from the fostering team within the local authority.

A positive viability assessment will then be progressed to the second stage, which is the full connected persons assessment. The whole process should not take more than 16 weeks and is governed by the Care Planning, Placement and Case Review Regulations 2010.

In addition to the care planning regulations, helpful guidance can be found in:

- Family Rights Group (2017) *Initial Family and Friend Care Assessment: A good practice guide on conducting viability assessments*. This document has been endorsed by the ADCS, CAFCASS and the Family Justice Council.

- *Family and Friends Care: Statutory guidance for local authorities* (2010). This sets out the framework for the provision of support to family and friends carers.

If the kinship carer or connected person is later granted a special guardianship order or child arrangements order, the child will lose the legal status of a child who is looked after.

21 Children looked after (CLA) reviews

The Children Act 1989 introduced for the first time in detailed regulations and guidance to local authorities the need to formulate and review care plans for children looked after by the local authority.

Each looked after child must have an appointed and named IRO before the child's first review (that is, within 20 working days, and within five weeks of coming into care) (s.25A Children Act 1989, amended by s.10 Children and Young Persons Act 2008). The child's care plan is reviewed independently by an IRO who chairs each review.

21.1 Independent Reviewing Officers

IROs, whether employed by the local authority or self-employed, maintain their independent status by being independent of the children's social work team and managed separately to children's services, usually as part of the quality assurance team or the chief executive department. This separation allows IROs to undertake independent scrutiny and oversight of the child's care plan. It also enables them to challenge poor practice and delay when reviewing care plans for looked after children. The *IRO Handbook* (DfE, 2010) is statutory, providing useful guidance on the roles and responsibilities of IROs.

After their first review, the care plan will be reviewed at the next review, three months after the child became looked after, and then every six months until the child ceases to be looked after. If deemed necessary, the frequency of reviews can be brought forward by the IRO, depending on the circumstances of the child's case. Consideration for a review will also be given if it is requested by the parents or the child, or if the child's placement is to be changed.

Issues that are discussed at the CLA review include:

- the effect of any change in the child's circumstances and care plan since the last review;

- whether previous decisions have been implemented and if not, why not;

- any necessary change in the child's legal status;

- contact arrangements and whether they are meeting the child's needs;

- the appropriateness of the current placement;

- whether any changes are needed to the placement plan;

- the wishes and feelings of the child, input by the parents and foster carers, and the views of the IRO about any aspect of the case, especially any changes since the last review and any proposed changes to the care plan.[130]

Each review will be recorded and is in two parts:

- Part 1 is completed by the child's social worker prior to the review meeting. It should record the impact of any actions or services provided to the child, and any changes.

- Part 2 is completed by the IRO as the Chair of the review, after evaluating how the current care plan is effectively meeting the needs of the child and whether

130 Care Planning, Placement and Case Review (England) Regulations 2010, schedule 7

any other changes are necessary, further to any information presented to the review.

21.2 Responsibilities of the IRO

The IRO will work in a collaborative way with the child's social worker, who is responsible for the looked after child. The IRO can offer a strong and positive direction to ensure that the child's care plan is being implemented, and will challenge where there is unnecessary drift or where the care plan needs to change, for example, the frequency of contact in line with the child's wishes.

The child's social worker should inform the IRO of any "significant failure" or significant changes to the child's care plan or of the child's circumstances.[131] The social worker should update the IRO of any outcomes from any meetings convened to consider the child's care plan or the child's care, such as changes in the child's permanence plan due to, for example, placement breakdown or an unplanned move. If a child's long-term care placement breaks down, then a review should be convened as soon as possible to consider the short- and long-term options for the child.

The role of the IRO is to:

- chair CLA reviews;
- endeavour to find out the child's views;
- monitor the appropriateness of the care plan;
- ensure that there is no drift or delay in carrying out the child's care plan;
- ensure that the care plan meets the needs of the child and, if it does not, to make representations on behalf of the child.

If the child is subject to a child protection plan, any child protection conference reviews should be co-ordinated prior to the CLA reviews, if possible, so that the protection plan can inform the review process.

131 Care Planning, Placement and Case Review (England) Regulations 2010, regulation 37(b)

If the child is subject to court proceedings, then the social worker should keep the IRO updated with the progress and of the final outcome of the proceedings. At the commencement of the proceedings, the social worker, when completing the social work evidence template, can include the IRO's view if known. During the proceedings, if considered necessary, the court can direct for the IRO's views to be filed in the court proceedings, which is another reason the child's social worker should keep the IRO informed of the proceedings.

The IRO has obligations to inform the child (having regard to the child's age and understanding) of their legal rights, including applications within the Children Act 1989 and of the complaints procedures, and to assist the child in obtaining legal advice (directly or indirectly).[132]

Local authorities have a duty to make arrangements for the IRO to have access to legal advice, should they wish to seek this on the child's behalf. If the child is subject to care or supervision proceedings, the IRO can also seek clarification, if required, from the local authority solicitor who has conduct of the proceedings.

21.3   The child's voice at the Looked After review

The legal framework for looked after children strengthens the responsibility of the IRO by ensuring that looked after children and young people are able to contribute effectively to their care planning. Section 26(2)(d) of the Children Act 1989 requires that the child's wishes and feelings will be sought at any Looked After Review. The IRO should speak to the child in private prior to each review so that they can personally establish the child's wishes and feelings and can then give due consideration to any views expressed by the child.

IROs play a key role in the care planning for children who are looked after. Their primary role is to review care plans and ensure that the child's wishes and feelings are given consideration and are, as far as possible, incorporated in the care plan with an overall aim to improve outcomes for children.

---

132 Care Planning, Placement and Case Review (England) Regulations 2010, regulation 45(1)

The heavy burden placed on IROs towards progressing the child's care plan was demonstrated in the case of *A and S v Lancs CC*.[133] In this case, two brothers, A and S, were removed as infants from their parents' care and placed in the care of the local authority. Both boys were freed for adoption in 2001 with the granting of freeing orders, with a care plan for adopted. (Freeing orders were introduced under ss.14–16 of the Children Act 1975. Once granted, such an order freed the child for adoption, which resulted in the parental rights and duties being transferred to the local authority's adoption agency. Freeing orders no longer exist, as a result of the Adoption and Children Act 2002, which replaced them with the introduction of placement orders.)

In 2004, the care plan for the children was changed from adoption to being placed in long-term foster care. By this time, A was aged seven and S aged six. No application was made to revoke the freeing orders, even though the care plan had now changed. If the local authority had done so, this would have meant that the local authority would have an obligation pursuant to s.34(1) and Schedule 3, paragraph 15(1) of the Children Act 1989 to promote reasonable contact with the children's mother and siblings.

The freeing orders meant that the children lost their links to their birth family, and for the next 11 years they were moved between a large number of foster placements; A was moved 77 times, and S 96 times. The children were physically and sexually abused in two of these placements. This resulted in them becoming more unsettled and disturbed. They did not have any contact with their birth family since 2002, despite their requests for contact.

In the 12 years that the children spent in care from 1999–2011, the IRO named in the case had chaired 16 reviews. The IRO accepted that he had failed to carry out his role, that he had not addressed or monitored the repeated failures of the children's social workers or protected A's and S's rights.

A was in foster care and the local authority wished to remove him from his placement. A wanted to remain in the placement and applied to the High Court for an order preventing the local authority from removing him. Further applications were made that the local authority and the IRO had breached the

133 *A and S v Lancs CC* [2012] EWHC 1689 (Fam)

children's rights under Articles 3, 6 and 8 of the EHCR. The local authority and the IRO accepted that they had breached these rights.

This case is a strong reminder, demonstrating the importance of the IRO's role for children who are looked after. Also, it reminds authorities that if a child's care plan changes from adoption, in that it is no longer considered to be the right plan for the child, the local authority should apply to revoke the placement order.

21.4 CAFCASS and IROs

There is an interesting relationship between CAFCASS and IROs, and the IRO's powers have been further clarified in an updated Practice Note (CAFCASS, 2017) issued by CAFCASS to explain the IRO's role in conjunction with CAFCASS.

CAFCASS officers will come into contact with IROs in two ways:

- when a child is looked after and is also subject to family proceedings;
- if the IRO considers it appropriate to refer the case to CAFCASS.[134]

Both of these scenarios are examined further.

- **When a child is looked after and is also subject to family proceedings**
  If the child is subject to care or supervision order proceedings, the Children's Guardian (who is a CAFCASS officer appointed by the court) and the IRO both play key roles. The Children's Guardian will consult with the allocated IRO as part of the Guardian's own ongoing analysis to ascertain whether the IRO has any concerns about the care planning process. The Children's Guardian will also liaise with the IRO, if considered necessary, to ascertain the child's wishes, the care plan and issues that may have been raised at court.

  Equally, the IRO should alert the Children's Guardian to any issues that may have arisen in the care planning and review meetings. This close liaison ensures that the child's voice can be heard and acted on in the court proceedings. At the conclusion of the proceedings, should the child remain looked after, the Children's Guardian should have a final discussion with the

134 S.25B(3)(a) Children Act 1989

child's IRO about the case with a view to identifying any outstanding issues from the court proceedings or other matters that should be kept under review.

- **If the IRO considers it appropriate to refer the case to CAFCASS**
  The IRO, in addition to seeking independent legal advice for the child, has also had the power since 2002[135] to refer a case of a looked after child to CAFCASS where the IRO considers it appropriate to do so.[136] This may be if the IRO has concerns about the child's care plan or the service that is being provided by children's services, or if perhaps the child's human rights have been breached and all attempts to resolve the matter have been exhausted. This right was extended in 2008[137] in that the IRO can refer a case to CAFCASS "if appropriate to do so", where there is failure in any "significant respect" in relation to the care plan, lack of implementation of decisions, or otherwise breach of duties by children's services in any material respect. The matter will only be referred to CAFCASS if the IRO has drawn these matters to the attention of senior managers within children's services and they have failed to address matters to the IRO's satisfaction within a reasonable time.[138]

The intention of this duty is to enable the IRO to have an effective independent oversight of the child's case and ensure that the child's interests are protected throughout the care planning process. It should be noted that it is extremely rare that the IRO will enforce this duty. It is more likely that any possible conflict will be resolved by escalating them to senior managers within children's services, which is usually successful in resolving any conflict over issues relating to the child's care plan between the IRO and the children social work team.

However, prior to consideration of any referral to CAFCASS, the IRO should consider whether it is possible to address matters by:

- the IRO engaging in discussions with the children social work team or accessing internal procedures within the local authority to resolve the dispute, such as escalating matters to senior management;

135 S.118 Adoption and Children Act 2002

136 S.25B(3)(a) Children Act 1989

137 S.25B(3) Children Act 1989

138 Care Planning, Placement and Case Review (England) Regulations 2010, regulation 45(3)

- the child making a complaint, either directly or with the assistance of an adult such as their foster carer, a children's rights officer or an advocate;

- the child or an adult on their behalf (such as their advocate) seeking independent legal advice to consider the legal options available to the child;

- the IRO speaking confidentially to a duty CAFCASS lawyer who is able to provide guidance but not legal advice. It should be noted that the guidance will only be on what steps may be available before the making of a formal referral to CAFCASS.

In most cases, it may be possible to resolve the matter; however, if it is not possible, a formal referral can be made to CAFCASS.

Before a formal referral is made by the IRO on behalf of the child, the IRO should consider the child's wishes and feelings and have regard to their age and understanding, giving due consideration to those wishes.[139]

Alternatively, where a child is of sufficient age and understanding and wishes to bring proceedings themselves, the IRO can assist the child in seeking independent legal representation.

Should the IRO wish to then pursue a formal referral to CAFCASS, the information should be shared with the relevant CAFCASS officer and the local authority. This referral process is only available to IROs. All other persons, such as the parents or child, need to follow other processes, such as a complaints procedure.

Examples of cases that can be referred to CAFCASS by the IRO are:

- unreasonable failure by a local authority to meet the statutory requirements for the looked after child. This could be matters such as delay in allocating a social worker or making timely visits to the child;

- unreasonable failure by a local authority to implement an essential element of the care plan, such as sibling contact or funding of a service or resource for the child;

- an unreasonable decision to move a child from a placement.

139 S.22(4) and (5) Children Act 1989

On receipt of the referral, CAFCASS will undertake a number of enquires, including ascertaining the child's views. It may attempt to settle the case through use of negotiation or mediation. It will also consider whether or not proceedings should be issued. On behalf of the child, CAFCASS can either commence judicial review proceedings or a free-standing application under the Human Rights Act 1998 by virtue of s.25B(3)(a) of the Children Act 1989. This process is positive for the looked after child as it will assist in progressing the child's matter and gives the IRO additional support; however, as already stated, it is rarely used.

This process should not be confused with the role of the Official Solicitor, as CAFCASS does not deal with compensation claims, which are within the Official Solicitor's remit. The Official Solicitor can conduct a wide range of civil cases on behalf of children and CAFCASS can refer cases to the Official Solicitor, if appropriate to do so. Examples of cases that the Official Solicitor would deal with are personal injury claims against the local authority where the claim is that a child has suffered harm due to the local authority's negligence.

21.5 The Lesland case: Part 11

Three days after the children were placed in foster care, Mrs Lesland (on Mr Lee's advice) telephones the out-of-hours duty social worker to state that she no longer consents to the children being voluntarily accommodated. Mrs Lesland states that she is going to visit the home of Caroline's foster carers and collect Caroline, as she and Mr Lee will now be caring for Caroline. Mrs Lesland says that given that Caroline is a baby, Mr Lee will not present a risk and therefore Caroline does not need to be in care.

Due to the reasonable cause to believe that all three children are likely to suffer significant harm, the social worker requests police assistance to place all three children under police protection to prevent their removal from foster care.

22   Police protection

Police protection is not an order, but a power granted to the police under s.46 of the Children Act 1989 for the removal and accommodation of children in cases of emergency.

> *s.46(1) Where a constable has reasonable cause to believe that a child would otherwise be likely to suffer significant harm, he may—*
>
> > *(a) remove the child to suitable accommodation and keep him there; or*
>
> > *(b) take such steps as are reasonable to ensure that the child's removal from any hospital, or other place, in which he is then being accommodated is prevented.*
>
> > *(2) For the purposes of this Act, a child with respect to whom a constable has exercised his powers under this section is referred to as having been taken into police protection.*

Police protection is an emergency administrative power, and there is no need to attend court as it is an administrative action taken by a police officer attending on the scene, after permission is granted by a senior police officer. As this is an administrative process, the parents' or the child's views are not obtained.

Police protection is reserved for situations where the police consider the child to be at risk of significant harm and the parents are unable to or are not co-operating with measures that the police consider necessary to safeguard the child, for example, agreeing for the child to stay with a relative or family friend. If the parents do not provide consent, then wherever possible the decision to remove the child from a parent should be made by the court. This is done by the local authority applying for an emergency protection order or interim care order. However, if it is an emergency and if the criteria are met, the police can remove the child or can take reasonable steps to prevent the child from being removed from, for example, a hospital or if the child is already in foster care or in the care of kin or connected persons.

In practice, if the child is to be removed to foster care, the police will contact the local authority for a foster placement to be located for them. Whilst the child is in police protection, the local authority will make the day-to-day decisions for the child. This will include consideration of reasonable contact with the parents, or anyone who has parental responsibility, or with whom the child was living when they were taken into police protection.

Police protection does not grant the police or the local authority parental responsibility. The duration of the police protection is limited to a maximum of 72 hours. This allows the local authority time to undertake an investigation and consider what further steps need to be taken to safeguard the child.

If the local authority considers that the child should not be returned to the parent's care for a further period of time due to the child having suffered or being at risk of significant harm, then the authority will firstly seek the parent's consent to the child remaining in foster care on a voluntary basis, under s.20 of the Children Act 1989. If consent is not forthcoming, then the local authority will need to consider applying for an emergency protection order or an interim care order on short notice.

However, if, on the expiry of the police protection, the matter does go to court, the court can scrutinise the use of the police protection, once proceedings are commenced. The court will consider the local authority's involvement in this process and if the authority requested the police to take out the police protection, it will consider whether there was proper use of this power.

22.1 The Lesland case: Part 12

The children were placed in police protection on Monday night, with the police protection due to expire on Wednesday.

The social worker meets with Mrs Lesland on Tuesday morning. Mrs Lesland informs the worker that she wants her children returned to her care, that Mr Lee is living with her and has proposed to her, and that they are in a committed relationship. She is very happy as they intend to get married, once her divorce with Mr Lesland is finalised.

Mrs Lesland does not agree to the children remaining in foster care and states that she would oppose any legal proceedings.

Given this information, the children's social worker seeks legal advice and the local authority applies for an emergency protection order before the expiry of the police protection. The social worker contacts Mr Lesland to inform him of the proceedings. He advises he does not want to be involved in any court proceedings and refuses to gives his address, as he also does not wish to receive any correspondence. The order is granted, as the local authority can evidence that the children are at immediate risk from Mr Lee. Prior to the expiry of the emergency protection order, the local authority commences care proceedings.

Public law proceedings

6

Public law proceedings are brought by the local authority on behalf of children's services to safeguard a child's welfare. If the child's welfare requires immediate protection, then an application can be made for an emergency protection order. If the proceedings are to be commenced in a more planned manner, then the local authority will apply for the commencement of care or supervision order proceedings. Both proceedings are discussed in this chapter.

1   Emergency protection orders

Any person can apply for this order; however usually it is the local authority. An emergency protection order (s.44 Children Act 1989) is applied for if it considers that the child is at imminent risk of significant harm. It can also be applied for without notice (*ex parte*) to the parents if there are sufficient grounds to warrant this course of action (s.44).

The court can grant an emergency protection order if it is satisfied that there is reasonable cause to believe that the child is likely to suffer significant harm:

- *if he or she is not removed into local authority accommodation; or*

- *if he or she does not stay in the place (such as a hospital or foster home), where he or she is currently being cared for.*

To proceed with the application, the local authority is required to give those with parental responsibility 24 hours' notice. The court can grant permission to proceed with the application on short notice should the court determine that this is necessary. The local authority can only pursue a short notice or a without notice application if the evidence can satisfy the court that providing notice to the parents or a person with parental responsibility could place the child at greater risk of harm.

Once the emergency protection order is granted, it lasts a maximum of eight days or fewer, and can be extended for a further seven days. In practice, however, orders will only be granted generally for a maximum of three days, giving the local authority sufficient time to issue care proceedings. The reason for this is that this is such a draconian order and a harsh measure for parents, particularly if the order was granted without notice to them. By only granting a short order, this enables the matter to come back to court at the earliest opportunity so that the parents can fully respond in the care proceedings, once commenced.

Once an emergency protection order is granted, the local authority acquires parental responsibility, which it shares with the parents. However, the local authority's exercise of parental responsibility is limited to the order's duration and only permits it to do what is reasonably required to safeguard or promote the child's welfare.

The court can make additional directions, such as for a medical or psychiatric examination or other assessments of the child or that there are no such examinations or assessments. It can also issue a warrant to permit a police constable to assist the social workers if they are likely to be prevented in the exercise of powers under this order.

Emergency protection order applications are a very serious step, and the court must be satisfied that it is both necessary and proportionate, and that there is 'no less radical form of order available'.[140] Due to the order's serious nature, if granted it will be an interference in the child's and family's family life (Article 8 ECHR). Helpful guidance on these orders can also be found in the statutory guidance (DfE, 2014)

140 Munby J, *X Council v B* [2004] EWHC 2015 (Fam)

Two leading cases provide clear guidelines for local authorities when considering applying for an emergency protection order: *Re X (Emergency Protection Orders)*[141] and the earlier *X Council v B (Emergency Protection Orders)*.[142]

In the case of *Re X (Emergency Protection Orders)*,[143] the Judge found significant flaws in the overall care proceedings, and in particular, the local authority's actions in obtaining an emergency protection order.

The case concerned care proceedings in relation to a nine-year-old child who had previously been subject to two child protection case conferences, with the child registered under the category of emotional harm. The third child protection case conference considered whether care proceedings should be commenced. After the conference, the social worker was informed that the mother had taken the child to a local hospital to be seen by a doctor. Within two hours, evidence was being given by the social work team manager in support of an application for an emergency protection order due to concerns relating to fabricated or induced illness. The application was made without notice to the parents and, once granted, the social worker, accompanied by four uniformed police officers, attended the hospital and removed the child from the mother's care to foster care, where she remained for 14 months.

The Judge found that there had been no emergency and quoted the Children Act Guidance and Regulations Volume 1 (p 51) (now replaced by statutory guidance (DfE, 2014)):

> *The purpose of the new order, as its name suggests, is to enable the child in a genuine emergency to be removed from where he is or be kept where he is, if and only if this is what is necessary to provide immediate short-term protection.*

---

141 *Re X (Emergency Protection Orders)* [2006] EWHC 510 (Fam)

142 *X Council v B (Emergency Protection Orders)* [2004] EWHC 2015 (Fam); [2005] 1 FLR 34

143 *Re X (Emergency Protection Orders)* [2006] EWHC 510 (Fam)

He continued: 'The words "genuine emergency" and "only what is necessary to provide immediate short-term protection" cannot, in my view, be stressed enough.'[144]

The Judge also found that at no stage in the proceedings did the local authority produce medical evidence to support the allegation of fabricated or induced illness. One year after the child had been in foster care, the local authority abandoned its reliance on the fabricated or induced illness claim and progressed the case based on emotional abuse.

The Judge found significant flaws and was highly critical of the social workers, and took the view that an emergency protection order should very rarely be used solely for the purpose of achieving some form of assessment or investigation.

To assist, the Judge in his judgement included a good practice guide incorporating the helpful summary set out by the Judge in the earlier case of *X Council v B (Emergency Protection Orders)*.[145] This guide is relevant in all applications for emergency protection orders:

1. An emergency protection order, summarily removing a child from their parents, is a "draconian" and "extremely harsh" measure, requiring "exceptional justification" and "extraordinarily compelling reasons". Such an order should not be made unless the court is satisfied that it is both necessary and proportionate and that no other less radical form of order will achieve the essential end of promoting the welfare of the child. Separation is only to be contemplated if immediate separation is essential to secure the child's safety, and "imminent danger" must be "actually established".

2. Both the local authority that seeks and the court that makes an emergency protection order assume a heavy burden of responsibility. It is important that both the local authority and the court approach every application for an emergency protection order with an anxious awareness of the extreme gravity of the relief being sought and a scrupulous regard for the European Convention rights of both the child and the parents.

---

144 *Re X (Emergency Protection Orders)* [2006] EWHC 510 (Fam), para 63

145 *X Council v B (Emergency Protection Orders)* [2004] EWHC 2015 (Fam); [2005] 1 FLR 34, para 57

3. Any order must provide for the least interventionist solution consistent with the preservation of the child's immediate safety.

4. If the real purpose of the local authority's application is to enable it to have the child assessed, then consideration should be given to whether that objective cannot equally effectively, and more proportionately, be achieved by an application for, or by the making of, a child assessment order under s.43 of the Children Act 1989.

5. No emergency protection order should be made for any longer than is absolutely necessary to protect the child. Where the order is made on an *ex parte* (without notice) application, careful consideration should be given to the need to ensure that the initial order is made for the shortest possible period, commensurate with the preservation of the child's immediate safety.

6. The evidence in support of the application for this order must be full, detailed, precise and compelling. Unparticularised generalities will not suffice. The sources of hearsay evidence must be identified. Expressions of opinion must be supported by detailed evidence and properly articulated reasoning.

7. Save in wholly exceptional cases, the parents must be given adequate prior notice of the date, time and place of any application by a local authority for an emergency protection order. They must also be given proper notice of the evidence upon which the local authority is relying.

8. Where the application for an emergency protection order is made *ex parte* (that is, without notice), the local authority must make out a compelling case for applying without first giving the parents notice. An *ex parte* application will normally be appropriate only if the case is genuinely one of emergency or other great urgency, and even then it should normally be possible to give some kind of albeit informal notice to the parents, or if there are compelling reasons to believe that the child's welfare will be compromised if the parents are alerted in advance to what is going on.

9. The evidential burden on the local authority is even heavier if the application is made *ex parte*. A local authority that seeks relief *ex parte* is under a duty to make the fullest and most candid and frank disclosure of all the relevant

circumstances known to them. This duty is not confined to the material facts; it extends to all relevant matters, whether of fact or law.

10. Section 45(7)(b) of the Children Act 1989 permits the court to hear oral evidence. However, it is important that those who are not present should nonetheless be made aware of what oral evidence and other materials have been put before the court. It is, therefore, particularly important that the court and the local authority representative 'keep a note of the substance of the oral evidence' and must also record in writing not merely its reasons but also any findings of fact. This is important in the event that the parents want to challenge this evidence in the care proceedings.

11. The local authority should inform the parents of exactly what has gone on in their absence. Parents against whom an emergency protection order is made *ex parte* are entitled to be given proper information as to what happened at the hearing if they ask, or provided with the panel's legal representation:

    a. copies of documents, bundles or other evidential materials lodged with the court either before or during the course of the hearing; and

    b. the legal authorities that were cited to the court.

12. Section 44(5)(b) of the Children Act 1989 provides that the local authority may exercise its parental responsibility only in such manner 'as is reasonably required to safeguard or promote the welfare of the child'. Section 44(5)(a) provides that the local authority shall exercise its power of removal under s.44(4)(b)(i) 'only...in order to safeguard the welfare of the child'. The local authority must apply its mind very carefully to whether removal is essential in order to secure the child's immediate safety. The local authority, even after it has obtained an order, is under an obligation to consider less drastic alternatives to emergency removal.

13. Consistent with the local authority's positive obligation under Article 8 to take appropriate action to reunite parent and child, s.44(10)(a) and s.44(11)(a) impose on the local authority a mandatory obligation to return a child who is subject to this order whom it has removed under s.44(4)(b)(i) to the parent from whom the child was removed if 'it appears to [the local authority] that

it is safe for the child to be returned'. This imposes on the local authority a continuing duty to keep the case under review day by day so as to ensure that parent and child are separated for no longer than is necessary to secure the child's safety. In this, as in other respects, the local authority is under a duty to exercise exceptional diligence.

14. Section 44(13) requires the local authority, subject only to any direction given by the court under s.44(6), to allow a child subject to an emergency protection order "reasonable contact" with their parents. Contact arrangements must be driven by the family's needs, not stunted by lack of resources.

Following the summary, the Judge provided additional good practice guidance[146] in relation to emergency protection orders which is still relevant:

a. The 14 key points made by the Judge in *X Council v B* should be copied and made available to the Judges/magistrates hearing an emergency protection order on each and every occasion that an application is made.

b. It is the local authority's duty to ensure that the *X Council v B* guidance is brought to the court's attention.

c. Mere lack of information or a need for assessment can never of themselves establish the existence of a genuine emergency sufficient to justify an emergency protection order. The proper course in such a case is to consider application for a child assessment order or issuing care proceedings under s.31 and seeking the court's directions under s.38(6) for assessment.

d. Evidence given to the court should come from the best available source. In most cases this will be from the social worker with direct case knowledge.

e. Where there has been a case conference with respect to the child, the most recent case conference minutes should be produced to the court.

f. Where the application is made without notice, if possible, the applicant should be represented by a lawyer, whose duties will include ensuring that

146 *Re X (Emergency Protection Orders)* [2006] EWHC 510 (Fam), para 101

the court understands the legal criteria required both for an emergency protection order and for an application without notice.

g. The applicant must ensure that as full a note as possible of the hearing is prepared and given to the child's parents at the earliest possible opportunity.

h. Unless it is impossible to do so, every without notice hearing should either be tape-recorded or be recorded in writing by a full note being taken by a dedicated note taker who has no other role (such as a clerk) to play in the hearing.

i. When the matter is before the court at the first "on notice" hearing, the court should ensure that the parents have received a copy of the notes of the emergency protection order hearing, together with a copy of any material submitted to the court and a copy of the Judge's reasons.

j. Cases of emotional abuse will rarely, if ever, warrant an emergency protection order, let alone an application without notice.

k. Cases of sexual abuse where the allegations are incohate and non-specific, and where there is no evidence of immediate risk of harm to the child, will rarely warrant an emergency protection order.

l. Cases of fabricated or induced illness, where there is no medical evidence of immediate risk of direct physical harm to the child, will rarely warrant an emergency protection order.

m. Justices faced with an emergency protection order application in a case of emotional abuse, non-specific allegations of sexual abuse and/ or fabricated or induced illness, should actively consider refusing the emergency protection order application on the basis that the local authority should then issue an application for an interim care order. Once an application for an interim care order has been issued, it is likely that justices will consider that the case should immediately be transferred up for determination by a Judge.

n. The requirement that justices give detailed findings and reasons applies as much to an emergency protection order application as it does to any other application. In a case of urgency, the decision may be announced and the order made with the detailed reasons prepared thereafter.

o. Where an application is made without notice, there is a need for the court to determine whether or not the hearing should proceed on a without notice basis (and to give reasons for that decision) independently of any subsequent decision upon the substantive emergency protection order application.

If the above guidance is not complied with, the local authority is unlikely to be able to proceed with its application.

In summary

- Emergency protection orders are draconian, must be proportionate and are only to be used where immediate and urgent risk to the child is identified.

- If the real purpose is for an assessment, then an emergency protection order is not appropriate, and perhaps a child assessment order may be more suitable.

- The order should be for no longer than is absolutely necessary.

- The application must be supported with detailed, precise and compelling evidence.

- Notice should be given to the parents, even if it is short or informal notice, unless it can be evidenced that this will place the child at greater risk.

- If parents or their legal representative do not attend the hearing for the emergency protection order, the parents should be provided with a copy of the order with a note of the court's reasons for making the order and the evidence presented to the court.

- After the order is granted, children's services should consider whether removal is still necessary, to keep the case under review and offer reasonable contact, or comply with any contact order granted at the time the emergency protection order was made.

Before the local authority can progress its application for an emergency protection order, given its draconian nature, the court legal adviser will require information as to what action has already been taken. This needs to be provided and the court legal adviser must be satisfied that an application for an emergency protection order should be progressed.

Information that the court will need to know is:

1. **Why is the local authority making this application?**

   - The local authority will need to provide the court details of the incident/injury or situation leading to the need for emergency protection.

   - The local authority needs to provide the evidence it relies on as to why it considers the child is at risk of significant harm.

   - What steps has the local authority taken so far to safeguard the child? If steps have not been taken, the court will need to know why.

2. **Has the child been subject to police protection?**

3. **Have the parents or anyone with parental responsibility been requested for consent for s.20 voluntary accommodation?**

   - The court will need to be informed of any attempts to get agreement for s.20 and/or an explanation of why s.20 is not suitable.

   - If the local authority's case is that informing the parents of the local authority's concerns may place the child at greater risk, how does the authority evidence this?

   - If time permits, the social worker should produce a brief statement detailing the local authority's evidence. In extreme emergencies, the court will allow applications without a statement. If this is the case, copies of police reports, referrals or the police protection notice, minutes of strategy meetings, child protection conferences, medical and psychiatric reports, if available, need to be produced at court in support of the authority's case.

Whichever way evidence is provided, it should fully support the application by being detailed and precise. Lack of evidence or generalities will not be accepted.

Any hearsay evidence must be identified, and the social worker's opinion must be supported by evidence and clear analysis. The court legal adviser will take a note of the social worker's oral evidence to be placed on the court file.

As previously stated, whilst the child is subject to an emergency protection order, the local authority must allow reasonable contact with their parents or any other person with parental responsibility. The court can also direct if contact is not to be permitted between the child and a named person.[147]

1.1 Lawful removal

A child can only be removed from the parent once the emergency protection order is granted. A reported case, that was highly publicised at the time, highlights this point. In this case,[148] a baby was removed from her mother, shortly after the mother had given birth, without either valid s.20[149] consent or an order. The mother was a care leaver, having been in the care of the same local authority and was now receiving leaving care services. The hospital took steps to remove the baby from the mother on behalf of the local authority, without receiving confirmation of the legality of the removal. The authority argued that, although consent had not been given, the mother had not objected to the removal.

The Judge found that simply because the mother had not raised an objection at the time did not mean that she had consented. In relation to the hospital, the Judge stated that it 'cannot immunise itself from liability by pleading the bare fact of "authority" allegedly "provided" by another public body'. The hospital staff should have checked that the local authority had lawful authority to remove the child before it acted on its behalf.

The court found that the removal was unlawful. The court relied on Article 8 of the EHCR and concluded that the interference with family life was not justifiable under Article 8(2) as a result.

147 S.44(6) Children Act 1989
148 *R (G) v Nottingham City Council* [2008] EWHC 152
149 Children Act 1989

The threshold (legal test) for applying for an emergency protection order is high, as can be demonstrated by the two cases below.

Case study 8: Protective measures

A mother was behaving strangely in the local park. She had with her her two-year-old daughter and was dancing by herself, whilst her daughter was watching her from the pushchair. When one of the other adults in the park approached the mother to ask her to stop dancing so near the other children, as she was frightening them, the mother responded by shouting in a threatening way. The police were called, and when they arrived the mother continued to behave strangely. The police attempted to approach the woman's daughter, as she was crying; the mother reacted by taking the child forcefully from the pushchair and holding her tightly, which made the child scream. The police were extremely concerned about the mother's mental health and placed her under s.136 of the Mental Health Act, and she was taken to a local mental health institution. The next day, she was discharged, as she was assessed not to be suffering from a mental health disorder but to have been under the influence of prescribed drugs, which she had taken with excessive alcohol, and to which she had had an extreme reaction.

Whilst the mother was in the mental health institution, the police placed the child under police protection under s.46 of the Children Act 1989. The child was placed in foster care. The local authority was not aware of the child until the police contacted them.

On the mother's release from the mental health institution, the local authority requested that the mother consent to the child remaining in foster care on the expiry of the police protection, until further assessment could be completed. The mother refused on the basis that her mother could be a protective factor by living in her home and supervising her. The checks were completed, and the maternal grandmother agreed to alert the police, should the mother's behaviour place the child at risk of harm. Both the mother and grandmother confirmed their agreement by signing the written agreement. The child was returned to the mother's home.

Children's services escalated the case to a child protection case conference where, through the protection plan and core group meetings, there would be further monitoring of the child's welfare.

This was an outcome that balanced the child's welfare with the mother's rights. An emergency protection order could not have been applied for as the local authority was not able to evidence the likely risk of signficant harm to the child, given that the maternal grandmother was a protective factor.

It is useful to contrast the case above with the one described below.

Case study 9: Emergency protection order refused

A mother, who was a failed asylum seeker, and her seven-year-old daughter came to the attention of children's services after a referral was made by her daugher's school, to whom the mother had disclosed that she believed her daughter had become possessed. When asked, the mother confirmed to the social worker that, as her daughter was possessed, she would have to engage in a ceremony to rid the spirits from her. The ceremony would involve making the child walk naked in their local church for the members of the church to smack her as she walked up and down the church aisle. The social worker was extremely concerned about the physical and emotional harm that the child would suffer. The social worker also believed that, if the mother became aware that the local authority was considering commencement of legal proceedings, she would flee from her accommodation. The mother had no ties to the area and appeared to have funds. The social worker was concerned about the mother's deteriorating mental health and advised her to see her GP. The mother became aggressive, and informed the social worker that once the exorcism of her daughter's spirits had been undertaken, she would be fine, as it was the spirits that were affecting her health.

The social worker requested that an application for an emergency protection order without notice to the mother be made. The social worker's view was that the child was at likely risk of significant harm and that, if the mother was given notice of this application, she would flee with the child and the child would then be at greater risk.

An immediate application was made for an emergency protection order without notice to the mother. The Judge was extremely concerned that the application had been made without notice and informed the local authority that the mother had to be given notice. It was explained to the Judge that the social worker feared that, as soon as the mother was given notice of the application, she would flee with the child. The Judge was not satisfied that the social worker could evidence this, and requested the local authority to manage the situation by putting protective measures in place to safeguard the child until this matter came before the court the next day at 10am.

The social worker went about trying to put in place protective measures. She visited the mother in the afternoon and informed her that an application would be made for an emergency protection order at court the next day. A taxi had been arranged to collect her and take her to court on the next day and a list of local solicitors was left for the mother to contact one. The social worker arranged to visit the mother and child again at 7pm on her way home and told her that she would meet her at court the next day. The social worker arranged for another worker from the emergency duty team to undertake a home visit at 9pm on the same day. The mother gave access to the social worker to enter her home and the child was observed to be sleeping in her bed.

The next day, the taxi arrived at the mother's home as arranged at 9am. The mother did not answer the door and it was found that she had disappeared with the child between 9.30pm the night before and 9am of the present day.

The local authority attended court and it was explained to the Judge that the mother and child had disappeared and that at present their whereabouts were unknown. The Judge's response was to immediately grant the emergency protection order. For the local authority the situation was critical, as it now had an order that granted parental responsibility for the child, whose whereabouts were unknown.

The social worker spent the rest of the day searching through the child's previous files to find any information as to where the mother could have gone. She found reference to a period of time that the mother had spent in Wales. She called numerous hospitals, social services departments and police in different parts of Wales, asking them to contact her should they have any sightings or contact with a woman and her seven-year-old daughter who did not appear to be local. Miraculously, a call was received the next day from a police station in a remote Welsh village that a woman and her daughter had been found. Within 24 hours, the child was brought back to the local area and placed in foster care.

The positive aspect of this case is that, with the support of the child's social worker, the mother received help to address her mental health and after a few months, her daughter was returned to her care.

This case demonstrates that, unless the concerns held by the local authority can be evidenced, the court is unlikely to permit an application without notice to proceed, as parents should be entitled to know what application the local authority is making in relation to their child.

2   Care proceedings

The Children Act 1989 has attempted to achieve a sound balance between, on the one hand, the parents' right to bring up their child in the best way they can and, if necessary, with local authority support as and when required. This is finely balanced with providing sufficient power to the local authority to enable it to intervene when necessary to protect a child who is at risk. The local authority can commence care or supervision order proceedings if it can establish the threshold criteria as set out in s.31 of the Children Act 1989, which means that the court will not make a care or supervision order unless it is satisfied.

s.31(2) Children Act 1989...

(a) that the child concerned is suffering, or is likely to suffer, significant harm; and

(b) that the harm, or likelihood of harm, is attributable to—

(i) the care given to the child, or likely to be given to him if the order were not made, not being what it would be reasonable to expect a parent to give to him; or

(ii) the child's being beyond parental control.

Evidence based practice is crucial in any proposed proceedings. Social workers will use their direct observations and evidence to form an understanding of what is going on for the child in their family setting. Social workers may be further assisted by research, peer review and supervision. This information will assist them to inform their analysis on the impact on the child, and to form a judgement on what is needed to resolve the identified issues.

The local authority, as the applicant, has the burden of proving to the court that the child has suffered or is at risk of suffering significant harm. This is known as the threshold criteria. The standard of proof required by the local authority is on a balance of probabilities. It is for the court to determine whether the threshold criteria have been met. The court undertakes this determination from the evidence that is presented by the local authority, and the other parties. The court will weigh up the evidence and on a balance of probabilities will make a decision as to whether the child has suffered or is at risk of suffering significant harm.

If the court is not satisfied that the local authority has proved its case, then the court cannot proceed with the case. This is unlikely to happen as the social worker will have sought legal advice from the local authority legal department and the court documents will only be submitted to court after the local authority lawyer has checked that the evidence being presented meets the required legal threshold as set out in s.31 of the Children Act 1989. The court cannot grant a care order in respect of a child who has reached the age of 17, or 16 if they are married.

If the care proceedings relate to a sibling group from the same household, the court must consider whether the threshold criteria have been satisfied in respect of each child. The court cannot grant a care order on one child simply because another child in the same household has been or is being ill-treated.

If the local authority is considering applying for a care order under the category that the child is beyond parental control, there is no requirement to evidence that there has been any failure on the part of the parent.

When the local authority is considering the commencement of care or supervision order proceedings under s.31 of the Children Act 1989, then it is required to apply the revised Public Law Outline (PLO), which is a child-focused procedural case management system with a statutory timescale of 26 weeks for completion of the proceedings.

The PLO includes a pre-proceedings stage that does not have a statutory timescale, although any unjustifiable delay will be open to scrutiny when the case goes before the court. The purpose of the PLO pre-proceedings stage is essentially to keep cases out of court by working with the parents to bring about a positive change, such that court intervention with the commencement of proceedings will not be necessary. To be successful, such a course of action requires the co-operation of the parents or family members to support the local authority's plan and engage in assessment and/or the services being provided by the authority during the pre-proceedings stage. This will only be embarked on if it can be ensured that the child is protected during this process.

There is no statutory timescale set down for the pre-proceedings stage; however, as recognised by the Public Law Working Group's interim report (2019), 'this process is not only about assessment, it is also about trying to effect change within the child's timescale'.

2.1 Family Drug and Alcohol Court

The Family Drug and Alcohol Court (FDAC) adopts what is sometimes referred to as the problem-solving approach; it deals with cases where the parent acknowledges that they misuse drugs or alcohol. The court conducts the care proceedings by co-ordinating a range of services to support the parent's holistic needs, which can also include support in relation to mental health, housing or a need for adult services to maintain care of their child or to have their child returned to their care.

It should be noted that the 26 weeks' PLO statutory timescale applicable in all care and supervision order proceedings is not applicable to proceedings that are being undertaken in the FDAC. Further information on the FDAC can be found at: www.fdac.org.uk.

2.2   Legal aid: Public law Children Act proceedings

Pre-proceedings

Once the local authority has provided the child's parents or carers with the 'letter before proceedings', the parent or carer with parental responsibility will be entitled to Level 2 legal help. This will entitle them to legal advice and the support of a solicitor during the pre-proceedings stage of the PLO, including attendance at the meeting with the local authority. The entitlement of Level 2 legal help is non means- or merit-tested.

Post commencement of proceedings

Should the local authority progress to commencing the application for a:

- care or supervision order;
- emergency protection order;
- child assessment order;
- secure accommodation order; or
- placement order;

the parent, carer or any party with parental responsibility will be entitled to fully funded legal representation, which will include advice and representation at court and entitlement to legal aid that is non means or non merit tested.

Once proceedings are commenced by the local authority, in addition to the parents, the child or children who are subject to the proceedings will also be parties. As the child lacks capacity to conduct their own legal proceedings due to their age, the court, on receipt of the local authority's application, will appoint a

Children's Guardian. A children's solicitor will also be appointed, whose fees will be funded with the issue of a legal aid certificate in the name of the child/ren. The child's entitlement to legal aid is non means and non merit tested.

If a party in the care proceedings does not have parental responsibility, such as a kinship carer, they will not be automatically entitled to legal aid. For a person in this situation, the solicitor will undertake an assessment of their means and merits. The merits are in relation to pursuing or defending the application. The means test is to consider whether the applicant is below the eligibility threshold of income or capital.

2.3 Extension of the 26 weeks

As already mentioned, the PLO is a case management system that is robustly adhered to by the judiciary. The 26-week time limit is the statutory timescale for all care and supervision order proceedings. It can only be extended if the court considers this to be necessary to enable the court to make its determination.

In *Re S (A Child)*,[150] the Judge detailed three contexts where an extension may be necessary:

1. A case that can be identified from the outset, or very early on, as one where it may not be possible to resolve the case justly within 26 weeks. Examples of such cases could be:

   a. cases where there is complex medical evidence, where a fact-finding hearing may be deemed necessary;

   b. cases in the Family Drug and Alcohol Court, requiring monitoring of drug or alcohol use;

   c. cases involving an international element, such as assessments of kinship carers who live abroad;

   d. cases where the parent's disabilities require recourse to special assessment or measures such as the invitation of the Official Solicitor (OS). The OS

150 *Re S (A Child)* [2014] EWCC B44 (Fam), para 33

only acts in cases in England and Wales, where there is no other person or agency that is able or willing to act for people who lack capacity (within the meaning of the Mental Capacity Act 2005), cannot manage their own affairs and are assessed as unable to represent themselves in proceedings. The OS acts as a litigation friend by providing instructions to the parent's solicitor on the parent's behalf. There is an informative Practice Note for solicitors which was updated in 2017 on the appointment of the Official Solicitor in Family Proceedings.[151]

2. Something unexpectedly arises that impacts on the proceedings, such as proposed carers withdrawing from offering care of the child, or related carers emerging later in proceedings who require assessment.

3. It is impossible to conclude the case justly within the 26 weeks due to failure on one or more of the parties. Having regard to the circumstances of the particular case, the court may consider that it is necessary to extend the time beyond 26 weeks to enable the court to resolve the proceedings justly.

Therefore, the general rule is that if the case cannot be justly concluded, an extension should be sought. This principle is encompassed in the words of the Judge in *Re NL (A Child) (Appeal: Interim Care Order: Facts and Reasons)*:[152] 'Justice must never be sacrificed on the altar of speed'.

To achieve the 26 week timescale with the best outcome for the child, it requires all professionals to play their key parts in the process, which means all the professionals, parties and their legal representatives working within the prescribed timescales.

The revised PLO aim is to streamline the public law process so that all care cases are concluded in 26 weeks, unless there are exceptional circumstances. So once proceedings are issued, it is the court that undertakes the case management responsibility by drawing up a timetable, but equally having regard to the impact the timetable will have on the child's welfare and conduct of the proceedings.

---

151 https://www.gov.uk/government/publications/appointment-of-official-solicitor-in-family-proceedings-practice-note

152 *Re NL (A Child) (Appeal: Interim Care Order: Facts and Reasons)* [2014] EWHC 270 (Fam)

Care or supervision order proceedings should only be commenced if the local authority can present evidence to meet the threshold criteria as set out in s.31 of the Children Act 1989. The courts have made it clear that what may be considered by others as imperfect parenting or perhaps "peculiar" ways of parenting would not be a reason alone to commence care or supervision order proceedings. The threshold must be established as set out in s.31. An important reminder was made in *Re A (A Child)*[153] of the temptation of social engineering and the need to recognise the inevitable diverse and unequal standards of parenting. In *Re A (A Child)*,[154] it cited the earlier judgement given in the case of *Re L (Care: Threshold Criteria)*:[155]

> Society must be willing to tolerate very diverse standards of parenting, including the eccentric, the barely adequate and the inconsistent. It follows too that children will inevitably have both very different experiences of parenting and very unequal consequences flowing from it. It means that some children will experience disadvantage and harm, while others flourish in atmospheres of loving security and emotional stability. These are the consequences of our fallible humanity and it is not the provenance of the state to spare children all the consequences of defective parenting. In any event, it simply could not be done.[156]

Another reminder is found in *North East Lincolnshire Council v G & L*;[157] the Judge stated:

> The courts are not in the business of providing children with perfect homes. If we took into care and placed for adoption every child whose parents had had a domestic spat and every child whose parents on occasion had drunk too much then the care system would be overwhelmed and there would not be enough adoptive parents. So we have to have a degree of realism about prospective carers who come before the courts.

153 *Re A (A Child)* [2015] EWFC 11
154 *Re A (A Child)* [2015] EWFC 11
155 *Re L (Care: Threshold Criteria)* [2007] 1 FLR 2050
156 *Re L (Care: Threshold Criteria)* [2007] 1 FLR 2050, para 50
157 *North East Lincolnshire Council v G & L* [2014] EWCC B77 (Fam)

Should the local authority wish to commence care or supervision order proceedings, it must bear in mind the need for evidence, analysis, the least interventionist approach, together with the local authority's general duty to promote the upbringing of children by their families, so far as this is consistent with its duty to promote children's welfare and avoid the need for proceedings where possible.

Once an application for care or supervision order proceedings is issued, the court has a two-stage process. Firstly, it must decide that the legal threshold criteria test as set out in s.31 of the Children Act 1989 is satisfied. Secondly, the court must apply the principle as set out in s.1(1) of the Children Act that the welfare of the child is the paramount consideration, having regard to the Welfare Checklist as set out in s.1(3) of the Children Act. Finally, before granting an order the court will also consider whether making an order is in the child's best interests rather than making no order, as set out in s.1(5) of the Children Act

The court is assisted by the social work evidence template document (SWET) that is completed by the social worker to support the local authority's application. In this document, the worker will set out the realistic options or orders for the child and why they are considered to be in the child's best interests as opposed to other options or orders.

2.4   Interim care and supervision orders

Care and supervision orders are governed by s.31 of the Children Act 1989; however, the court will not make a final order until all the evidence has been put before it. Until such time, the court can make an interim care order under s.38 of the Children Act 1989, if it is satisfied that there are reasonable grounds for believing that the child's circumstances are as mentioned in s.31(2) of the Children Act 1989. This is governed by s.38(1):

Where—

(a) *in any proceedings on an application for a care order or supervision order, the proceedings are adjourned; or*

(b) *the court gives a direction under section 37(1),*

the court may make an interim care order or an interim supervision order with respect to the child concerned.

(2) A court shall not make an interim care order or interim supervision order under this section unless it is satisfied that there are reasonable grounds for believing that the circumstances with respect to the child are as mentioned in section 31(2).

The Children and Families Act 2014 amended the Children Act 1989 in that an interim care order will last for however long the Judge decides. In practice, it is usually until the next hearing or a further order.

The granting of an interim care order should not be regarded as placing the local authority at an advantage over the parents. The order enables the local authority to share parental responsibility (subject to any restrictions imposed by the court) with the parents with parental responsibility.

If an interim care order is not deemed necessary, then in accordance with the No Order Principle under s.1(5) of the Children Act 1989, an order will not be made. This may be because the parents are co-operating. This can act as supportive evidence of the parents' continued co-operation with the authority for the duration of the proceedings.

2.5   Public Law Outline

As already mentioned, care or supervision order proceedings have a statutory timescale of 26 weeks, governed by specific stages of the PLO, as follows:

- Stage 1: undertaken between one–two days from the day of the local authority's application being issued by the court.

The case will be listed for a contested interim care order, if the local authority is seeking an interim care order and this is opposed by the parents. If this is not opposed, then the court will list the case for a case management hearing.

- Stage 2: a case management hearing, undertaken between 12–18 days. Prior to this hearing, there will be a meeting of the advocates, involving all the parties' legal representatives. The purpose of this meeting and the case management hearing is to progress the timetable of the case by deciding on the filing dates of evidence. The case will be listed for the next hearing, which is the issues resolution hearing.

- Stage 3: the issues resolution hearing, undertaken by not later than week 16–20 from the date of the application. There will be an advocates' meeting arranged between the legal representatives at least two days before this hearing. The purpose of this meeting and hearing, as the title suggests, is to resolve issues and if possible to use this hearing as a final hearing. If matters cannot be resolved, then the case will be listed for a final hearing.

- The final hearing will be listed before week 26. If the case requires it, then the court can consider granting permission to go beyond 26 weeks if necessary to do so.

  (1) The court will draw up a timetable for the proceedings with a view to disposing of the application –

  (a) without delay; and

  (b) in any event within 26 weeks[158]

The key stages of the PLO pre-proceedings and after commencement of proceedings are detailed in the PLO flowchart in Appendix 4.

2.6   Fact-finding hearing

In cases where there is a clear factual issue to be determined, the court may decide to conduct a threshold hearing, also called a "split hearing" or a "fact-finding hearing". This type of hearing is considered necessary where the child's final care plan cannot be determined without the resolution of some issue of fact. The court will consider whether the child's interests require the fact-finding hearing, which could, for example, relate to allegations of a child having been physically or sexually abused. The effect of this hearing is that there will be an early identification of the issues to be tried in relation to the threshold criteria.

---

158 Practice Direction 12A, para 5.1

Where a fact-finding hearing is necessary, there are two stages, the first being the causation hearing; that is, who caused the harm and who was the perpetrator? If this is not possible to determine, the court may resolve matters by determining whether the parent failed to protect the child and whether they will be unable to do so in future. The second stage requires consideration of future risk. At the conclusion of the process, the court will make findings in relation to the threshold criteria.

Once the threshold criteria are satisfied, the court will then consider the child's care plan and what order to grant. If the child's interests are not served by the granting of an interim care order or care order, the court can consider a lesser order in accordance with the least interventionist principle during or at the conclusion of the proceedings.

If the evidence is not based on a single issue, such as a non-accidental injury or sexual abuse, then the threshold can be based on the number of issues, which may include, for example, an injury to the child, but also neglect. In these types of cases, the whole of the threshold criteria can be determined at the final hearing as a composite hearing. The Judge in the case of *Cambridgeshire County Council v PS & Others* stated:[159]

> *The use of split hearings must be confined to those cases where there is a stark or discrete issue to be determined and an early conclusion on that issue will enable the substantive determination (i.e. whether a statutory order is necessary) to be made more expeditiously.*

2.7   Care orders

Once a care order is granted, the local authority becomes the child's corporate parent. The care order cannot be conditional or limited in any way. This was confirmed by the Court of Appeal in the case of *P-S (Children)*.[160] In this case, the Judge had made what was termed a short-term order, to allow the local authority to test the children's placements with their respective carers.

159 *Cambridgeshire County Council v PS & Others* [2014] EWCA Civ 25, para 27
160 *P-S (Children)* [2018] EWCA Civ 1407

The Court of Appeal clarified that the concept of a short-term order is flawed.

> There is no mechanism for a care order to be discharged on the happening of a fixed event or otherwise to be limited in time. The exercise of parental responsibility by a local authority cannot be constrained once a full care order is made other than on public law principles of unlawfulness, unreasonableness and irrationality...[161]

The care order will last until the child's 18th birthday, unless it is discharged earlier. The application for discharge can be made by the local authority, anyone with parental responsibility, and even the child themselves.[162]

2.8   Supervision orders

This order places the child under the local authority's supervision. The duty of the supervisor from the designated local authority is to:

- advise, assist and befriend the child for the duration of the order;

- take such steps as are reasonably necessary to give effect to the order;

- where the order is not wholly complied with or if the supervisor considers that it may no longer be necessary, to consider whether or not to apply to the court for its variation or discharge.

This order can last from up to one year and be extended for a further two years, before expiry of the original order. The order can have requirements attached, requiring the responsible person, that is, the person with parental responsibility or with whom the child is living, to take certain action. However, the conditions may not be imposed without the responsible person's consent, as the order requires a co-operative working relationship between the local authority and the parents/carers with parental responsibility. The supervision order does not grant the authority parental responsibility and therefore the local authority is unable to enforce compliance with the conditions.

---

161 *P-S (Children)* [2018] EWCA Civ 1407, para 33
162 S.39(1) Children Act 1989

2.9 Care plan

Local authorities have a statutory duty to provide a care plan in the care and supervision order proceedings.[163] The care plan is devised following the child's social worker's assessment and will detail the local authority's plan for meeting the child's needs. The plan acts as a safeguard, requiring the local authority to set out what its proposed plan is for the child, which should then be implemented when the care or supervision order is made. If the court is not satisfied with the plan, it can make an interim order until it is ready to endorse a satisfactory care plan. When local authorities are presenting the care plan in care proceedings, consideration should be given by the authority at an early stage to rehabilitation, that is, return of the child to their parents' care. Alongside this plan, the authority is also required to consider other permanency plans running simultaneously to avoid delay in permanency planning for the child's future care arrangements. This process is often referred to as twin tracking, parallel planning or concurrent planning. It can include assessment of kinship or connected persons, or plans for adoption or placement with Fostering for Adoption carers.

Two leading cases have had a substantial impact on the way in which the courts expect local authorities to present their evidence and care plans.

Re B (A Child)[164]

In this case, the local authority's care plan was adoption. The plan to rehabilitate the child to the parents' care had been ruled out on the basis that the child would be likely to suffer significant harm in the future. The Supreme Court emphasised the need for the local authority to consider all support that could be offered to the family in order that the child could remain in the parents' care care due to the draconian nature of a care plan for adoption, 'a very extreme thing, a last resort', only to be made where 'nothing else will do'.

163 S.31A Children Act 1989, as amended by s121 Adoption and Children Act 2002
164 *Re B (A Child)* [2013] UKSC 33

Re B-S (Children)[165]

In this case, the Judges were critical of the care plan in that it lacked analysis by the local authority:

> *We have real concerns, shared by other judges, about the recurrent inadequacy of the analysis and reasoning put forward in support of the case for adoption, both in the materials put before the court by local authorities and guardians and also in too many judgements. This is nothing new, but it is time to call a halt.[166]*

These cases did not change the law, as was confirmed in the later case of *Re R (A Child)*.[167] What did change was the landscape in the way local authority evidence is to be provided to the court. The requirement is for local authority social workers to provide a statement supporting the care plan, containing an analysis of all the realistic options and why the authority supports the option it is recommending over and above other options. To support local authorities in submitting what became known as *Re B-S* compliant evidence, a social work evidence template (SWET) was devised in 2014 to guide workers as to what information the court requires.

2.10 Children's Guardian

In care or supervision order proceedings, the child who is subject to the proceedings becomes party to the proceedings, and as such is entitled to legal representation and the appointment of a children's solicitor. As the child is a minor, their children's solicitor will take instructions from the court-appointed Children's Guardian, unless the child is deemed to have capacity to be able to instruct their children's solicitor.

CAFCASS is responsible for providing the Children's Guardian service to the courts. The Guardian's role is to look at the case and consider matters and the

---

165 *Re B-S (Children)* [2013] CIV 1146
166 *Re B-S (Children)* [2013] CIV 1146, para 30
167 *Re R (A Child)* [2014] EWCA Civ 1625

evidence from the perspective of what is in the child's best interests. The court is entitled to give weight to the Children's Guardian's recommendations.

Should conflict arise between the Children's Guardian and the child, and if the child has capacity to instruct the solicitor directly, then the children's solicitor will separate from the Children's Guardian. This means that the children's solicitor will take instructions directly from the child and the Children's Guardian will continue to provide to the court what they consider to be in the child's best interests.

2.11   Contact

When a child is in care, the local authority has a duty to promote contact with anyone who is significant to the child.[168]

If there is disagreement about contact arrangements, the issue can be resolved by the making of a contact order for a child in care under s.34 of the Children Act 1989. Section 34(1) states that if a child is in care, the local authority shall allow them to have reasonable contact with their parents, guardian, with those who have parental responsibility, and/or had care of the child prior to their coming into care. The contact can include face-to-face direct contact or indirect arrangements such as by letter or telephone.

If the local authority considers that any form of contact would not be in the child's best interests, it can apply for an order under s.34(4) for permission to refuse contact with the person named in the order. However, if, after the granting of this order, the authority decides that contact can now be offered, it can facilitate contact without the need to go back to court.

Where a local authority has decided to refuse contact on an emergency basis due to safeguarding reasons, the authority can suspend contact for seven days.[169] The local authority must make an application to court for permission to refuse further contact before the expiry of the seven days, requesting a contact order under s.34(4) of the Children Act 1989, for permission to refuse further contact with a named person. As already mentioned, this order permits the authority to refuse

168 Schedule 2, para 15(1) Children Act 1989
169 S.34(6) Children Act 1989

contact between the child and the named person. Should circumstances change, and the local authority later agree for contact to be reinstated, then the authority can facilitate this without the need to return to court.

The Lesland case: Discussion

The local authority's care plan is for all three of Mrs Lesland's children to remain in foster care, pending further assessments. The authority plans to issue care proceedings to seek interim care orders in respect of all three children, and for them to remain in foster care due to the risks Mr Lee poses to them, given their mother's decision to continue with the relationship.

For the court to endorse this care plan, the local authority has to first satisfy the court that the risk of harm meets the threshold criteria as set out in s.31 of the Children Act 1989. The least interventionist approach and the No Order Principle need to also take into account the children's welfare. The local authority has to show why it needs to share parental responsibility with the parents and why an interim care order is the necessary order, as opposed to any other less interventionist order available under the Children Act 1989.

2.12   The Lesland case: Part 13

Care proceedings have commenced. Mr Lesland is contacted and restates that he does not wish to be involved in the proceedings. He informs the children's social worker that he supports his mother to care for Caroline, should it not be possible for her to be cared for by her mother.

Mr Gill is located and served with notice of the proceedings. He informs the social worker that Mrs Lesland had made it difficult for him to see Rachel and Josh once she had met Mr Lesland. Mr Gill instructs a solicitor and requests to become involved in the proceedings. He is made a party to the proceedings and he wishes to be assessed as a long-term carer for Rachel and Josh.

The parenting assessment of Mrs Lesland is negative and concludes that she is not able to prioritise the children's needs over her relationship with Mr Lee, and that, if the children are returned to her care, they are likely to be at risk of sexual abuse.

At the final hearing of the care proceedings, Mrs Lesland confirms through her solicitor that she is not willing to leave Mr Lee and does not accept the risks he poses to her children.

During the proceedings, Mr Gill is reintroduced to Rachel and Josh initially for the purpose of contact. Mr Gill then states that, given Josh's needs and that Rachel and Josh should be together, he cannot look after the children long term. The social worker speaks with Mr Gill and explains that the local authority can consider providing support to him to care for the children, but Mr Gill says it is too much to take on.

Mrs Price puts herself forward to be a long-term carer for Caroline and wants to apply for a special guardianship order. Further to a positive viability assessment of Mrs Price, Caroline is placed with her as a kinship carer. The local authority commences a special guardianship assessment of Mrs Price. Unfortunately, before the assessment is completed, Mrs Price withdraws from the process, as she does not feel that she can commit to caring for Caroline long term.

No other family members come forward for any of the children.

Care proceedings are concluded within the 26 weeks as required by the PLO. Care and placement orders are granted in respect of all three children. The placement orders give the local authority permission to place the children in an adoptive placement. Further to a sibling assessment, the court approves the care plan for Rachel and Josh to be placed together and if an adoptive family cannot be identified within six months, they will remain in foster care with their current carers. The care plan for Caroline is to be placed in a separate adoptive placement.

Mrs Lesland is to have supervised contact with the children, given her ongoing relationship with Mr Lee. Once Caroline is placed with her adoptive parents, Mrs Lesland will have a farewell contact visit. Thereafter, she will have letterbox contact twice a year. There will also be sibling letterbox contact four times a year.

3 Permanency orders

3.1 Special guardianship orders

Special guardianship orders were introduced further to the Government's review of adoption in 2000. The Government recognised a need for an alternative legal status for children that offered greater security than long-term fostering but without the absolute severance from the birth family that stems from an adoption order. This resulted in the introduction of special guardianship orders in the Adoption and Children Act 2002 (s.115), introducing new sections 14A–14G in the Children Act 1989, creating a new type of legal order that gives permanence and security to those children who could not achieve this via other legal routes.

Special guardianship orders are intended for children who cannot live with their birth parents, but can be cared for by extended family members or friends known (connected) to the family. This is a private law order that grants the holder/s, known as special guardians, parental responsibility for a child until they reach the age of 18. The making of the order does not extinguish the parents' parental responsibility but allows the special guardian to exercise parental responsibility to the exclusion of any other person (with the exception of any other special guardian) with parental responsibility for the child. It therefore allows the special guardian/s to make day-to-day decisions on the child's behalf.

There are limitations on the special guardian's exercise of parental responsibility, including that they may not give consent for a child to be adopted, cannot change the child's surname, or make arrangements for a child to live outside the UK for more than three months without the written consent of each parent who has parental responsibility or with the court's permission.

3.2 Placement orders

A local authority is unable to place a child in a prospective adoptive placement unless those with parental responsibility have consented, or if the court decides to dispense with the consent of those who have parental responsibility and grants a placement order.

A placement order[170] is a public law court order that authorises the local authority to place a child for adoption with any prospective adopters. It remains in force until it is revoked, the child is adopted, or the child reaches the age of 18. In practice, if a child is not placed in an adoptive placement within nine months of the granting of the placement order, the local authority should consider making an application to the court to revoke the order and change the child's care plan.

Once granted, this order suspends any care or supervision order and transfers the parental responsibility to the adoption agency, giving it the ability to restrict the parental responsibility of the child's parents. When the child is placed, parental responsibility is also given to the prospective adopters; however, the adoption agency will determine to what extent parental responsibility is delegated to them in order for them to exercise it.

3.3   Placement orders and contact

Section 26(2)(a) of the Adoption and Children Act 2002 makes clear that, if a placement order is made, no application may be made for a child arrangements order for contact under s.8 of the Children Act 1989, and no application may be made for a contact order under s.34 of the Children Act 1989.

If a contact order is to be made, then s.26(2)(b) of the Adoption and Children Act 2002 permits the court to make an order for contact between the subject child and any person named in the order:

S.26(2)(b) Adoption and Children Act 2002

The court may make an order under this section requiring the person with whom the child lives, or is to live, to allow the child to visit or stay with the person named in the order, or for the person named in the order and the child otherwise to have contact with each other.

Section 26(3) of the Adoption and Children 2002 lists those who can apply for a s.26 contact order as of right and all others, who must first obtain the court's

170 S.21 Adoption and Children Act 2002

permission before applying. In addition, s.26(4) permits that the court may on its own initiative make a contact order under s.26 of the Adoption and Children Act:

> *S.26(4) When making a placement order, the court may on its own initiative make an order under this section.*

Section 27 makes further consequential provision as to contact under a placement order:

> *S.27(4) Adoption and Children Act 2002:*
>
> *(4) Before making a placement order the court must:*
>
>> *(a) Consider the arrangements which the adoption agency has made, or proposes to make, for allowing any person contact with the child, and*
>>
>> *(b) Invite the parties to the proceedings to comment on those arrangements.*
>
> *ss.26 and 27 of ACA 2002 require the court in every case before making a placement order to consider the proposed arrangements for contact and the views of the parties as to those arrangements. The court is given wide and flexible powers to make arrangements for contact between the child and any other person in the period prior to any placement for adoption and until an adoption order is granted.*

A placement order continues in force until it is either revoked by the court (ACA 2002, s.24), or an adoption order is granted with respect to the child or the child marries, forms a civil partnership or attains the age of 18 years (ACA 2002, s.21(4)). A contact order made under s.26 may, therefore, cover a relatively short period between the making of a placement order and the subsequent granting of an adoption order. Or, potentially for far longer periods in the event an adoptive placement cannot be identified as the power of the court to make an order under s.26 is not confined to the occasion of the child's placement with prospective adopters and therefore extends to the entire period "while" an adoption agency is authorised to place, or a child is placed, for adoption (ACA 2002, s.26(2)).

3.4 Adoption orders

An adoption order,[171] once granted, transfers parental responsibility to the adopters and permanently extinguishes the parental responsibility of anyone who had parental responsibility immediately before the making of the order. Once the adoption order is made, the adopted child is deemed to be the adopter's legitimate child and in law will be regarded as if they had been born to the adopter/s. This change means that the birth parents lose all their legal status as parents of the child and no longer retain any of the rights or responsibilities they previously held. Also, the making of the adoption order will result in the adopted child no longer being recognised as a legal member of the birth family and will also lose all inheritance rights. In the event a child who is to be adopted also may be entitled to any property or assets from a deceased birth family's estate, it is advisable for specialist legal advice to be obtained on the child's behalf in relation to any potential inheritance rights prior to the final adoption order being granted.

Before making an adoption order, the court must consider whether there should be arrangements allowing any person contact with the child, or whether any existing contact should continue. In order to consider this, the court will obtain the views of the parties to the proceedings.[172]

3.5 Post-adoption contact

Section 9 of the Children and Families Act 2014 inserts a new s.51A and s.51B in the Adoption and Children Act 2002. The court has the ability to make an order for contact or to prohibit contact when either making an adoption order or after one has been made. These provisions can assist adoptive parents who perhaps wish to prevent or stop informal contact, for example, via social media.

Section 51A of the Adoption and Children Act 2002 specifically allows for individuals to make applications for post-adoption contact if they are related to the child, and this includes step-parents, siblings and foster carers.

The Act identifies categories of people who can be named in such orders:

171 S.46(1) Adoption and Children Act 2002
172 S.46(6) Adoption and Children Act 2002

- a person who, prior to the adoption, was related to the child by blood or half blood, marriage or civil partnership;

- a former guardian of the child;

- any person who had parental responsibility immediately before the adoption order was made;

- any person with whom the child lived for one year, which does not need to be continuous but does need to be within five years before the application is made.

When these provisions were first introduced, they raised a certain level of anxiety from adoptive parents that, with the increase of categories of people, this would lead to an increase of applications for contact orders. This has not been the case.

Section 51A(4)(c) of the Adoption and Children Act 2002 requires that anyone seeking an order for post-adoption contact must obtain the court's permission to pursue their application. When considering the application, the court will consider:

- the applicant's connection with the child, adopter or prospective adopter;

- any risk the proposed application may have on disrupting the child's life; and

- any representations made to the court by the child or adoptive family.

The case of *Re B (A Child) (Post-Adoption Contact)*[173] was the first to receive judicial consideration on the issue of post-adoption contact since implementation of the Children and Families Act 2014. In this case, the Court of Appeal considered whether an order should be made for an adopted child to have continuing contact with their birth family after they are adopted. Sir Andrew McFarlane, President of the Family Division, gave the leading judgement and made it clear that the legislation may be different, but the court's approach remains the same; that is, making a contact order requiring adoptive parents to allow contact with the child's birth parents will only be made in exceptional circumstances. The President

---

173 *Re B (A Child) (Post-Adoption Contact)* [2019] EWCA Civ 29

stressed that the law set out in *Re R*[174] is still applicable in relation to applications for post-adoption contact:

> *The imposition on prospective adopters of orders for contact with which they are not in agreement is extremely, and remains extremely, unusual.*[175]

The approach taken in *Re R* was cited with approval by the Court of Appeal in the case of *Oxfordshire County Council v X, Y and J.*[176] These proceedings related to a girl, J, born in January 2007, and aged three at the time of the appeal hearing. J was the subject of an adoption order that had been made by the same Judge on 7 April 2009. The question that the Judge had to determine at the hearing which was the subject of this appeal was whether, as the birth parents wished, there should be an order requiring the adoptive parents to provide them annually with a photograph of J. Or whether, as the local authority, the adoptive parents and J's Children's Guardian contended, the adoptive parents should make the photograph available for viewing by the birth parents at the local authority's offices. The Judge decided in favour of the adoptive parents and dismissed the application for a contact order made by the birth parents;

> *It is a strong thing to impose on adoptive parents, it is "extremely unusual" to impose on adoptive parents, some obligation which they are unwilling voluntarily to assume, certainly where, as here, the adoption order has already been made...the adoptive parents were genuine when they expressed their concerns, so what was the justification for imposing on them something they conscientiously and reasonably objected to, particularly when, as we have seen, they say that they have not ruled out the possibility of letting the birth parents have photographs in the future?*[177]

This approach in *Re R* and the Oxfordshire case was reiterated in *Re B*[178] by the President:

---

174 *Re R* [2005] EWCA Civ 1128
175 *Re R* [2005] EWCA Civ 1128, para 49
176 *Oxfordshire County Council v X, Y and J* [2010] EWCA Civ 581
177 *Oxfordshire County Council v X, Y and J* [2010] EWCA Civ 581, para 36
178 *Re B (A Child) (Post-Adoption Contact)* [2019] EWCA Civ 29

> *The law remains...that it will only be in an extremely unusual case that a court will make an order stipulating contact arrangement[s] to which the adopters do not agree.*[179]

> *Save for there being extremely unusual circumstances, no order will be made to compel adopters to accept contact arrangements with which they do not agree.*[180]

In the case of *Re B*,[181] the child was placed in a Fostering for Adoption placement, and therefore was already living with the prospective adopters but as a foster placement, as the care and placement orders had not been granted. The prospective adopters and birth parents knew each other. The birth parents were both disabled in respect of their intellectual functioning, the birth mother being very significantly disabled. In the adoption proceedings, the birth parents sought ongoing direct contact with the child for one hour, twice a year. The prospective adopters opposed this but were agreeable to a face-to-face meeting once a year between the birth parents and themselves, with the proviso that the child could be included in these meetings sometime in the future, 'once a trusting relationship had been established'.

The Judge, when making the adoption order, refused to make a contact order under s.51A of the Adoption and Children Act 2002. The birth parents appealed. The Court of Appeal agreed with the earlier decision that a s.51A contact order would not be in the child's welfare.

The Court of Appeal, when considering this case, also noted that the purpose of s.51A of the Adoption and Children Act 2002 was 'with the aim of reducing the disruption that inappropriate contact can cause the adoptive placements'.

Although the substantive appeal was refused in *Re B*,[182] the Court of Appeal was asked to consider providing further guidance on the issue of post-adoption contact. The President clarified that summary in the judgement detailed below

179 *Re B (A Child) (Post-Adoption Contact)* [2019] EWCA Civ 29, para 59
180 *Re B (A Child) (Post-Adoption Contact)* [2019] EWCA Civ 29, para 62
181 *Re B (A Child) (Post-Adoption contact)* [2019] EWCA Civ 29
182 *Re B* [2019] EWCA Civ 29

was a matter of social work practice guidance and was not something that was required in law for every case.

The summary in relation to post-adoption contact is as follows:

1. *Adoption agencies should ensure that all prospective adopters and all adoption social workers fully understand the developing research when undergoing training and approval;*

2. *In every case where post-adoptive contact is a realistic option, the local authority should file, during the placement proceedings, the best information available as to the pool of "open" adopters nationally and to ensure this is as specific to the subject children as possible;*

3. *The social worker and children's guardian to consider the significance of the research studies in every case;*

4. *The court to provide full reasons in determining any contact application under s.26 Adoption and Children Act 2002;*

5. *Sibling contact to be considered as an entirely separate exercise from parental contact;*

6. *For there to be an open and frank dialogue between social workers, prospective adopters and birth parents and, if sufficiently mature, siblings about the child's needs, possibly with a face-to-face meeting as in this case.*

4   In care

4.1   Education support for children in care

As discussed previously, all children who are looked after must have a care plan. This is drawn up and reviewed by the local authority responsible for the child. The care plan must include a health plan and a Personal Education Plan (PEP).

The PEP will detail plans that need to be undertaken to help the child to fulfil their potential academic progress and meet their educational needs.

The Children and Social Work Act 2017 expanded the role of Virtual School Heads and designated teachers to children who are looked after or who were previously looked after, and now includes children who have left care and are now subject to adoption, special guardianship or child arrangements orders.

4.2 Virtual School Heads

The Virtual School Head (VSH) is a senior officer within the local authority. They are in charge of promoting the educational achievement of all children who are looked after by the local authority and those children who have left care and are now subject to adoption, special guardianship or child arrangements orders. As part of their responsibilities, they make information and advice available to parents/carers and the school.

4.3 Designated Teachers

For children who are looked after, the school has a duty to appoint a designated staff member to have responsibility for promoting their educational achievement. They will also be the central point of initial contact and will take lead responsibility within the school. The designated teacher should have lead responsibility for helping school staff to understand the issues that can affect how children who are looked after learn and achieve. Statutory guidance is available on the role and responsibilities (DfE, 2018).

4.4 Pupil Premium Plus

Children who are looked after, or who have left care through adoption, special guardianship or a child arrangements order, are eligible for Pupil Premium Plus funding. This is provided to help improve the educational attainment of children who are looked after or who were previously looked after. The Department of Education produced statutory guidance in 2018.

4.5   Education, Health and Care Plan

The Children and Families Act 2014 created a new "birth-to-25-years" Education, Health and Care Plan (EHCP) for children and young people with special educational needs. This replaces the special education needs process, and the new process offers families personal budgets so they have more control over the type of support required.

4.6   Independent visitors

Children and young people in care who have lost contact with their birth family can feel isolated and perhaps have no one to turn to outside the local authority or their foster carers to represent their interests.

In the case of a child who has not been visited by a parent or a person with parental responsibility for a period of 12 months, or where communication has been infrequent, the local authority can consider the appointment of an independent visitor. The child or young person is consulted and, if they object, the appointment will not be progressed.

The independent visitor will be independent of the local authority and can be known to the child or be a stranger. They will be required to make regular visits to the child and also maintain contact, by telephone and letter as appropriate. The purpose of their contact is to:

- befriend the child;
- give advice and assistance as appropriate with the aim of promoting the child's development and social, emotional, educational, religious and cultural needs;
- encourage the child to exercise their rights and participate in decisions that will affect them;
- support the care plan for the child;
- complement the activities of the carers.

4.7   Children's rights officers and advocates

The importance of listening to children has already been discussed in this guide, along with the fact that this can help to safeguard children and protect them from harm. Advocacy can do the same, however, it can also have the effect of empowering children and young people to ensure that their rights are respected and their views and wishes are heard. This is particularly important not just for children who are looked after, but also for those who are about to leave care.

In addition to IROs, looked after children also have the right to access the assistance of a children's rights officer. This officer's services are provided by local authorities, which are required to have an advocacy service for children in care.[183] Local authorities can either provide this service in-house or contract services externally from independent children's rights organisations such as the National Youth Advocacy Service (NYAS) or Coram Voice. Whether in-house or external, these services are independent and confidential, and the children's rights officer will provide information, advice, advocacy, representation and support to the child.

An appointment of a children's rights officer or an advocate can be made, for example, where the child wishes to be represented at a meeting or assisted in making a complaint. For a younger child, a foster carer or independent visitor could access the services of a children's rights officer on behalf of the child.

---

183 S.26A Children Act 1989, inserted by s.119 Adoption and Children Act 2002

Leaving care

7

1   The Lesland case: Part 14

Adoptive placements could not be identified for Rachel and Josh. The IRO agrees to the change of care plan to long-term foster care and this is approved by the agency decision-maker in the local authority. The authority applies to revoke the placement orders. Rachel and Josh remain in the care of their foster carer.

Caroline is placed with prospective adopters, who apply for an adoption order.

Six years later, Rachel is now approaching 18, and wishes to remain in foster care until she finishes her A Levels. The local authority agrees to Staying Put arrangements (see below).

Rachel plans to go to university and seeks support from the local authority to pursue her plans; she is provided with support under the leaving care provisions.

Rachel wishes to access her records to understand why she and Josh ended up in foster care. She is supported by her social worker to do this.

2   Staying Put and Staying Close arrangements

2.1   Staying Put

The Children and Families Act 2014[184] introduced a new duty on local authorities in England to advise, assist and support fostered young people to stay put with their foster families post the young person's 18th birthday until their 21st birthday, if

184 S.98 Children and Families Act 2014 inserted s.23CZA Children Act 1989

both parties agree. Upon reaching 18, the child in foster care is no longer a looked after child but is recognised as an adult, a care leaver and a former relevant child (if they have been in foster care for 13 weeks or more) under the leaving care provisions. Once Staying Put arrangements are in place, the placement transfers from being a foster placement to Staying Put arrangements, and is governed by leaving care legislation and statutory guidance and not the fostering services regulations.

The benefit of Staying Put arrangements is that these provide continuity of support and placement during a crucial period in a young person's life as they transition to adulthood. This situation also more closely replicates the experience of young people who remain with their birth families.

Children's social workers and IROs should consider Staying Put arrangements as part of the continuum of care. The young person should be consulted as part of the care planning process, which should happen as early as possible and preferably by their 16th birthday. Should the young person decide that Staying Put is not right for them, support should be provided to consider alternative arrangements such as supported or independent accommodation.

As part of the preparation for adulthood, the child's social worker will liaise with the allocated personal adviser who will take over supporting the young person once they reach the age of 18.

2.2 Staying Close

Staying Put is a statutory provision that supports young people to continue to live with their former foster carers. However, there is no statutory equivalent provision for young people leaving residential care.

Sir Martin Narey considered this issue in his report on children's residential care (2016). He found that young people leaving children's homes require as much support as those leaving foster care and recommended the introduction of a similar provision to Staying Put, calling it "Staying Close", designed for young people leaving residential care. This would allow the young person to have the continued support of the same team and key worker from the residential home and the ability to visit the home frequently.

The Government has made a commitment to introduce Staying Close. The scheme was piloted first in order to understand the costings, practicalities and impact. The Government has now given £10m to boost the Staying Put and Staying Close schemes in 2020/21 as part of the package of additional support for care leavers. This will include funding for a national roll-out of Staying Close in 2021/22.

3 Leaving care/after care services

As part of the local authority's corporate responsibilities, local authorities have a statutory responsibility to ensure that all young people in their care are provided with support and services to help with the smooth transition to adulthood, just as any good parent would do for their own child.

These "after care provisions" were inserted in the Children Act 1989 by the Children (Leaving Care) Act 2000, 'to help young people who have been looked after by a local authority move from care into living independently'.[185]

These provisions, together with the enactment of the Children and Young Persons Act 2008, are designed to prevent a young person who has been looked after by a local authority being cut off suddenly from local authority support past their 18th birthday. The effect of this is that the young person has the provision of support and services post 18 years from their corporate parent. The local authority that looked after the young person is known as the "responsible authority".

There are four categories that will determine whether the young adult is entitled to leaving care services:

- **Non eligible care leaver:** this is a child who left local authority care before their 16th birthday. These children will not be eligible for leaving care services.

- **Eligible child:** this is a young person who is aged 16 or 17 and has been looked after for a period in total of at least 13 weeks, which began after their 14th birthday and ended after their 16th birthday. It is the duty of the local authority

185 Children (Leaving Care) Act 2000, explanatory note to the 2000 Act, para 5

looking after an eligible child to advise, assist and befriend them with a view to promoting their welfare when they cease to look after them.

For each eligible child, the local authority must carry out an assessment of their needs with a view to determining what advice, assistance and support would be appropriate for them to provide while they are still looking after them, and after they cease to look after them, and will then prepare a pathway plan for them. The pathway plan has to be kept under regular review. A local authority must arrange for the child to have a personal adviser.

- **Relevant or qualifying child:** this is a young person aged 16 or 17 who was looked after for a period of at least 13 weeks, which began after their 14th birthday and ended after their 16th birthday, but who has now left care (or would have been relevant but for the fact that they were detained through the criminal justice system, or were in hospital, on their 16th birthday). The local authority has a duty to take reasonable steps to keep in touch with a relevant child for whom it is the responsible authority, whether they are within their area or not. To appoint a personal adviser and if no pathway plan has already been prepared, the authority must carry out an assessment of the child's needs with a view to determining what advice, assistance and support it would be appropriate for them to provide and prepare a pathway plan for the young person. If a relevant child returns home and stays there for six months, they cease to be a relevant child. However, if this arrangement breaks down before their 16th birthday, they return to being a relevant child.

- **Former relevant child:** this is a young person who is now aged 18 plus and who was an eligible or relevant child. The local authority has a duty to give a former relevant child assistance to the extent that their welfare and educational or training needs require it, in kind or, in exceptional circumstances, in cash until they reach the age of 21, or longer if their pathway plan sets out a programme of education or training that extends beyond their 21st birthday.

The leaving care provisions require the local authority to undertake an assessment of an eligible child not later than three months after the child becomes 16. Some authorities may commence this assessment from the time the young person turns

13 or 14. More defined and supportive processes apply to children with a disability who may not be able to move on to independence as young adults.

The young person, once they become 18, no longer has a social worker. From 18 years onwards, the young person, if eligible for leaving care services, will have a personal adviser. As part of the transition process, it is important that the personal adviser is introduced as early as possible to the young person and definitely before the end of the social worker's involvement, to assist the young person to form a relationship with their personal adviser..

When the young person reaches 18, they no longer have a care plan but a pathway plan. The child's social worker will work closely with the personal adviser and the young person in completing the assessment in order to formulate the young person's pathway plan, prior to the young person's 18th birthday.

The assessment will identify what support and services the young person will require for them to successfully reach independence, such as cooking or budgeting skills. The social worker will ensure that the young person's foster carer is also part of this process so that the young person can be supported in the foster care placement. The earlier this process commences, the more beneficial it is for the young person and their path to independence, and also facilitates a smooth transition from the social worker to the personal adviser.

The assessment will include:

- health and development;

- education and training or employment plans;

- support available to the young person from family or other persons;

- financial needs;

- the skills the young person possesses necessary for independent living;

- the young person's needs for care, support and accommodation.

The Government has recognised that leaving care can be difficult and has taken proactive steps to improve the support available to young people leaving care by introducing a new duty in the Children and Social Work Act 2017.[186] Changes introduced by this Act require local authorities to now provide all care leavers with the support of a personal adviser up to the age of 25, if they wish to access this support, irrespective of whether the young person is engaged in education or training. This includes care leavers who return to the local authority at any point after the age of 21, up to the age of 25, and who request support.

This new duty also introduced two other related provisions in the Children and Social Work Act 2017:

- a duty on local authorities to consult on and then publish their "local offer" for care leavers, which sets out both care leavers' legal entitlements and the additional discretionary support that the authority provides; and

- a duty on local authorities that requires them to have regard to seven "corporate parenting principles", set out in s.1(1) of the Children and Social Work Act 2017, that will guide the way in which the authority provides its services to children in care and care leavers.

Pursuant to the passing of the Children and Social Work Act 2017, the DfE produced key statutory guidance, *Promoting the Education of Children in Care and Previously Looked After Children* (2018a), and *Extending Personal Adviser Support to all Care Leavers to age 25* (2018b).

4   Role of the personal adviser

The personal adviser is not a social worker, but a professional worker who will have hands-on experience of supporting young people to undertake practical steps, such as completing forms and setting up bill payments. The personal adviser will use the pathway plan to identify steps that the young person needs to take to achieve their goals and how the local authority will support them to do so.

The personal adviser will:

- provide personal and practical advice and support to the young person;

---

186 S.3 Children and Social Work Act 2017

- review the pathway plan;

- liaise with the responsible authority over implementation of the pathway plan;

- co-ordinate the provision of services and make sure that the young person can make use of such services;

- maintain contact with the young person.

- keep informed about the young person's progress and well-being; and

- keep written records of contact with the young person.[187]

5   Pathway plan

The pathway plan is effectively an agreed plan between the young person and the local authority as to what their needs are, what their future plans are, and how the local authority will support them to meet those needs and fulfil the plans.[188] It will set out a career pathway with milestones such as education, training or support that the young person will require.

If the young person fails to engage with their social worker or is unco-operative in the formation of the pathway plan, this does not permit the local authority to not devise a detailed pathway plan. This was clearly established in *R (on the application of J) v Caerphilly*:

> *The fact that a child is uncooperative and unwilling to engage, is no reason for the local authority not to carry out its obligations under the Act and the Regulations. After all, a disturbed child's unwillingness to engage with those who are trying to help is often merely a part of the overall problem which justified the local authority's statutory intervention in the first place. The local authority must do its best.[189]*

The pathway plan will include:

187 Regulation 12, Children (Leaving Care) (England) Regulations 2001
188 Paragraph 22, explanatory notes to Children (Leaving Care) Act 2000
189 *R (on the application of J) v Caerphilly* [2005] EWHC 586 (Admin), para 56

- the accommodation to be provided to the young person;

- a plan of education or training, or the support the young person will be provided with to seek employment;

- the support the young person will require in developing and sustaining family relationships;

- a programme to develop personal and practical skills the young person requires for independent living;

- the financial support that will be provided by the local authority to the young person post 18 years old;

- the young person's health needs, and this may include mental health needs and how these will be met;

- any contingency plans for action if the pathway plan does not work.[190]

6   Young person's participation

The young person should be invited to participate in any meetings so as to ensure that their views and wishes are considered in the formulation of the pathway plan. The young person should be provided with a copy of the pathway plan or any review and the contents should be explained to them.[191]

The personal adviser must stay in touch with the young person. The frequency of the meetings will be dependent on the young person's needs.

If the young person fails to agree to meet, the personal adviser must use their best endeavours to keep in touch, including informing the young person of how they can re-engage with the service should they wish to do so.

If the young person is not satisfied with the service, they are entitled to make a complaint. Section 24D of the Children Act 1989[192] requires every local authority to establish a formal process for dealing with complaints from care leavers.

190 Schedule to the Children (Leaving Care) (England) Regulations 2001
191 Regulation 6, Children (Leaving Care) (England) Regulations 2001
192 Inserted by the Children (Leaving Care) Act 2000

7 Access to social work records

An essential element of good professional practice is for social workers to maintain social work records, which should include:

- decisions, clearly recording by whom and when and how they were made;

- records of information received from other professionals or persons;

- evaluations, assessments and analysis of information.

Local authorities must ensure that records are stored safely and can be retrieved promptly and efficiently. Local authorities have a retention policy that will set out how long they will keep records depending on what record it is and what the final outcome was for the child. If the child was looked after in foster care, or in a children's home, the local authority's children's services will retain a child's social care files up to the 75th anniversary of the child's birth. If the child died before age 18, records will be retained for 15 years from the date of death.[193] If the child is adopted, the adoption file will be retained by the adoption agency for at least 100 years from the date of the adoption order.[194] For other situations, the policy will determine how long the files are retained for.

The case of *C, R (On the Application of) v Northumberland County Council*[195] highlights the need for retention of records for long periods. This was an application for judicial review by the claimant, who had been subject to a child protection investigation. The claimant's view was that he and his family had been the subject of a significant injustice in their dealings with the local authority and he sought the destruction of the case records. The authority's retention policy required child protection records to be retained for 35 years after case closure.

The claimant also sought an order quashing the policy and/or a declaration that it was unlawful. The application was dismissed. The court held that the

---

193 S.50 Care Planning, Placement and Case Review (England) Regulations 2010, and regulation 36, Children's Homes (England) Regulations 2015

194 Regulation 6, Disclosure of Adoption Information (Post-Commencement Adoptions) Regulations 2005

195 *C, R (On the Application of) v Northumberland County Council* [2015] EWHC (Admin) 2134

local authority policy was in accordance with the law and had been carefully considered and adapted. It was applied proportionately and flexibly. The court accepted that the purpose of retaining the records went beyond the local authority's defence of claims against it, that there was a need to keep the record for a significant period of time as it served the purpose of protecting other children, allowing those whose data was retained to access it later in life, and to make it available, if necessary, in cases of later investigation, enquiries or litigation.

Children can request access to information held about them. Access will be given depending on their age, and capacity to understand and deal with the process. Generally, children over the age of 13 or 14 are considered competent to make applications for their records or to give permission for others to see their records.

Parents or carers who have parental responsibility can request disclosure of their child's records. However, if the child is considered competent then their views will be sought, including their right to confidentiality, which will be given proper consideration.

If the child is in the care of the local authority, an application for disclosure can be made to the child's social worker. If the young person has left the care of the local authority, then application for disclosure can be made to the local authority's data protection officer or access to records officer.

Records that will not be disclosed to the child are as follows:

- records held about other people who have not consented to their personal data being shared or disclosed;

- information from third parties unless they are a relevant person, such as a nurse, social worker or doctor, or if they have given their permission;

- information that is considered to be seriously harmful to the young person;

- records relating to legal proceedings, (unless the young person was a party to the proceedings); and

- information held to prevent or detect crime, or to prosecute offenders, where the request for the information is likely to affect either, or both, of these purposes.

A complaint can be made in relation to any decision for refusal of records.

8   What if a local authority "fails" in its duty of care?

If the local authority is believed to have failed in its statutory duties, there are a number of ways in which a complainant can take action in relation to that failure.

8.1   Complaints procedure

The complaints procedure comes under s.26 of the Children Act 1989. It has three separate stages.

- **Stage 1: Complaint:** This stage starts with the making of a complaint to the allocated child's social worker, social work team or complaints officer within the local authority. It can be submitted orally or in writing. A response should be received within 10 working days from the child's social worker's manager or a manager from children's services. If the complainant is not satisfied, they can request their complaint to proceed to Stage 2.

- **Stage 2: Formal Investigation:** This stage requires children's services to appoint an investigating officer who is responsible for undertaking an investigation of the complaint. This is done in consultation with the independent person, who is also appointed by children's services to oversee the process and ensure that it is carried out fairly. The report is then submitted to a senior manager within children's services to consider and to make a decision about the complaint in writing. This process should be completed within five weeks. This period of time can be extended if the matter is complicated. The complainant can request a copy of the investigator's report. If still not satisfied with the outcome, the complainant can proceed to Stage 3.

- **Stage 3: Review Panel:** Children's services will arrange a panel of up to three independent members. They must then arrange for the panel to meet within 30 working days to hear the complainant and children's services in an open and fair way. Within five working days, the panel will provide a written report with their recommendations, which can include particular actions for children's services and payment of compensation to the complainant. A senior member of children's services will make the final decision as to what action will be taken within 15 days of the panel's report. If the decision is not to follow all or any of the panel's recommendations, good reasons need to be provided.

8.2 Local Government Ombudsman

If the complainant is still not satisfied, further to Stage 3 of the complaints process, then a complaint can be made to the Local Government Ombudsman (LGO) about decisions and inactions by children's services in relation to their duties and powers under the Children Act. The LGO can investigate further. It will only do so once all complaints procedures within the local authority have been exhausted. If findings are made by the LGO, it can award damages to be paid by the authority. The LGO publicises its decisions on its website, naming the local authority.

8.3 Judicial Review Proceedings

An application can be made to the High Court requesting the Judge to review the lawfulness of the local authority's decision, action or failure. The grounds are that the local authority did not apply the law correctly, that the decision or action is irrational or unfair. The purpose of this application is not to consider the merits of the decision but whether the process or the action taken was correct. Before an application is made, the applicant first has to apply for permission to pursue the application for Judicial Review. If the applicant is successful, the High Court can quash, that is, cancel the decision or grant an order, requiring the local authority to take or not to take action.

8.4 Action for the local authority's negligence

There have been a number of successful cases that have resulted in awards of damages being paid to claimants for a local authority's failure in carrying out their statutory responsibilities. One such case is *Jake Pierce v Doncaster Metropolitan Borough Council*,[196] in which the Court of Appeal upheld a decision of the High

196 *Jake Pierce v Doncaster Metropolitan Borough Council* [2008] EWCA Civ 1416

Court to award damages to the claimant against the local authority for failing to take Jake into care as a child.

The local authority can be held responsible for failures by their employees and even foster carers. *Armes v Nottinghamshire County Council*[197] established that if a child is a victim of abuse whilst in foster care, they can bring an action for damages against the local authority. In this case, the claimant was taken into care at seven years old. She was placed in her first foster placement for four years and was found to have been physically and emotionally abused by her foster mother. One year later, in another foster placement, the court found that she had been sexually abused by her foster father. The local authority was found not to be negligent in the selection or supervision of the foster carers. The issue was whether it was liable for the abuse the claimant suffered perpetrated by the carers.

The Supreme Court held that that the local authority was held vicariously liable. As a result of this leading case, foster carers are now treated in the same way as employees of the local authority when considering a claim.

The decision in *Poole Borough Council v GN & Another*[198] is a landmark judgement that has clarified the law in relation to the extent that a local authority's duty of care is to protect children in their area, in the exercise of its child protection functions. In this case, it was found that the local authority did not owe a duty of care to protect children from harassment by neighbours. The claimants, now adults, claimed that when aged seven and nine, they had been placed together with their mother in housing adjacent to another family who, to the local authority's knowledge, had persistently engaged in anti-social behaviour. The nine-year-old was severely disabled and was receiving services from children's services on a "child in need" basis.

The family became a target of harassment and abuse that persisted over several years. It included vandalism of the mother's car, attacks on the family home, threats of violence, verbal abuse, and physical assaults on the mother and younger child. The younger child expressed suicidal thoughts and was allocated

197 *Armes v Nottinghamshire County Council* [2017] UKSC 60
198 *Poole Borough Council v GN & Another* [2019] UKSC 25

the same social worker as his elder brother, and the mother was referred to mental health services.

These incidents were reported to the local authority and it was decided that the family be rehoused away from the estate. The mother and children moved into their new home in December 2011.

The claimants argued that the abuse and harassment they suffered from May 2006 to December 2011 had caused them physical and psychological harm, and that the local authority was liable for its negligent failure to exercise its social services functions to protect them from harm caused by third parties. The claimants further argued that, if the whole family could not be moved, the children should have been removed from the family home into at least temporary care under the Children Act 1989. They argued that there was a direct duty of care owed to them in common law, deriving from the local authority's Children Act duties, including sections 17, 20 and 47.

The Supreme Court concluded that there was no arguable assumption of responsibility; and that the local authority did not owe a duty of care to these children in relation to the performance of their social services functions.

On the issue of whether the claimants should have been removed as children, under s.31(2) of the Children Act, the court clarified that it would be necessary to establish that the claimants were suffering, or were likely to suffer, significant harm that was attributable to a lack, or likely lack, of reasonable parental care. The threshold criteria could not be met in this case as the harm suffered by the claimants was attributable to the conduct of the neighbouring family, rather than a lack of reasonable parental care. Therefore, there were simply no grounds for removing the children from their mother.

Conclusion

It is clearly established that a child protection system based on defensive and anxious systems can have the impact of an increase in care proceedings and consequently the looked after population. In line with the principles of the Children Act and in particular with regards to the least interventionist approach, this is not what should be aimed for. A successful system enables social care professionals to have the capacity to form trusting relationships so that they can undertake robust and analytical assessments within the necessary time. These assessments will inform the child's short- and long-term needs and how these can be met. This, in turn, will enable decisions to be made in a supportive and manageable way, resulting in many more successful journeys for children travelling through the looked after system, with better outcomes. This in turn enables these children to transition into successful adulthood, which will benefit them when they become the next generation of parents, carers or social care professionals.

As said at the start of this guide, the UK is known to have one of the most advanced and successful child protection systems. However, the success of systems very much depends on the professionals working within them. For that reason, social care professionals and those supporting children have a responsibility to have greater awareness and understanding of the application of the law and good practice. The aim of this book is to arm the reader with knowledge of the law and practice to enable them to support children to have a positive and successful journey through care.

References

International Instruments

- European Convention for the Protection of Human Rights and Fundamental Freedoms 1950 (ECHR)
- United Nations Convention on the Rights of the Child 1989 (UNCRC)

Legislation

- Adoption and Children Act 2002
- Care Act 2014
- Children Act 1975
- Children Act 1989
- Children Act 2004
- Children and Adoption Act 2006
- Children and Families Act 2014
- Children (Leaving Care) Act 2000
- Children and Social Work Act 2017
- Children and Young Persons Act 2008
- Civil Partnership Act 2004
- Criminal Justice and Court Services Act 2000
- Data Protection Act 2018
- Equality Act 2010
- Family Law Reform Act 1969
- Guardianship of Infants Act 1925
- Human Fertilisation and Embryology Act 2008

- Human Rights Act 1998
- Legal Aid, Sentencing and Punishment of Offenders Act 2012
- Local Authority Social Services Act 1970
- Marriage (Same Sex Couples) Act 2013
- Mental Capacity Act 2005
- Mental Health Act 1983
- Offences Against the Person Act 1861
- Prevention of Cruelty to, and Protection of, Children Act 1889
- Powers of Criminal Courts (Sentencing) Act 2000
- Surrogacy Arrangements Act 1985

Statutory Regulations/Statutory Instruments

- Breaks for Carers of Disabled Children Regulations 2011
- Breaks for Carers of Disabled Children Regulations 2011
- Care Planning, Placement and Case Review (England) Regulations 2010
- Children (Leaving Care) (England) Regulations 2001
- Children (Leaving Care) Act 2000 Regulations and Guidance
- General Data Protection Regulation (EU) 2016/679
- Family Procedure Rules 2010
- Fostering Services Regulations 2002
- Short Breaks for Carers of Disabled Children Regulations 2011

Statutory Guidance

- Children Act 1989: Guidance and Regulations: Volume 2: Care Planning, Placement and Case Review, 2010
- Children Act 1989: Guidance and Regulations: Volume 1: Court Orders, 1991
- Court Orders and Pre Proceedings for Local Authorities, April 2014
- Disclosure of Adoption Information (Post-Commencement Adoptions) Regulations 2005
- Family and Friends Care: Statutory Guidance for Local Authorities 2010
- IRO Handbook Statutory Guidance for Independent Reviewing Officers and Local Authorities on their Functions in Relation to Case Management and Review for Looked After Children, December 2010

- Promoting the Education of Looked After Children and Previously Looked After Children: Statutory guidance for local authorities, February 2018
- Short Breaks for Carers of Disabled Children, March 2011
- The Designated Teacher for Looked After and Previously Looked After Children: Statutory guidance on their roles and responsibilities, February 2018
- Working Together to Safeguard Children: A guide to inter-agency working to safeguard and promote the welfare of children, July 2018

Good practice guides

- *CAFCASS Practice Note 2017*, December 2017
- *Guidelines for Judges meeting Children who are Subject to Family Proceedings*, Family Justice Council, April 2010
- *Guidance for Solicitors appointing the Official Solicitor*, 2017
- *Initial Family and Friend Care Assessment: A good practice guide*, Family Rights Group, 2017
- *Recommendations to Achieve Best Practice in the Child Protection and Family Justice Systems, interim report*, Public Law Working Group, June 2019
- *Recommendations to achieve Best Practice in the Child Protection and Family Justice Systems: Special guardianship orders*, Public Law Working Group, June 2020

Case law

- *A v United Kingdom [1998] 2 FLR 959, Times 1/10/98, ECHR*
- *A and S v Lancs CC [2012] EWHC 1689 (Fam)*
- *Armes v Nottinghamshire County Council [2017] UKSC 60*
- *B v A & Others (Parental Responsibility) [2006] EWHC 2 (Fam)*
- *Behre & Ors, R v Hillingdon & Anor [2003] EWHC 2075 (Admin)(HC)*
- *CA (A Baby) [2012] EWHC 2190 (Fam)*
- *Cambridgeshire County Council v PS & Others [2014] EWCA Civ 25*
- *Coventry City Council v C, B, CA and CH [2012] EWHC 2190 (Fam)*
- *C, R (On the Application of) v Northumberland County Council [2015] EWHC (Admin) 2134*

- *CW v SG [2013] EWHC 854 (Fam)*
- *Gillick v West Norfolk & Wisbech Area Health Authority [1986] AC 112*
- *Gurgulu v Germany [2004] 1 FLR 894*
- *Hewer v Bryant [1970] 1 QB 357, para 369*
- *Jake Pierce v Doncaster Metropolitan Borough Council [2008] EWCA Civ 1416*
- *Johansen v Norway [1997] 23 EHRR 33*
- *Kent County Council v M & K (s.20 Declaration & Damages) [2016] EWFC 28*
- *M v M (Child Access) [1973] 2 ALL ER 81*
- *North East Lincolnshire Council v G & L [2014] EWCC B77 (Fam)*
- *Northamptonshire County Council v AS & Others [2015] EWHC 199*
- *Oxfordshire County Council v X, Y & J [2010] EWCA Civ 581*
- *PM v MB & Anor [2013] EWCA Civ 969*
- *Poole Borough Council v GN & Another [2019] UKSC 25*
- *P-S (Children) [2018] EWCA Civ 1407*
- *R (G) v Nottingham City Council [2008] EWHC 152*
- *R (On the Application of B) v London Borough of Merton [2003] EWCH 1689*
- *R (On the Application of J) v Caerphilly [2005] EWHC 586 (Admin)*
- *R (On the Application of A) (FC) v LB Croydon [2009] FCR 317, [2009] UKSC 8*
- *Re A (A Child) [2015] EWFC 11*
- *Re B [2019] EWCA Civ 29*
- *Re B (Role of Biological Father) [2008] 1 FLR 1015*
- *Re B (A Child) (Care Order) [2013] UKSC 33*
- *Re B (A Child) (Post-Adoption Contact) [2019] EWCA Civ 29*
- *Re B-S (Children) [2013] Civ 1146*
- *Re C (Children: Contact) [2002] 3 FCR 183, [2002] 1 FLR 1136*
- *Re C and V (Contact and Parental Responsibility) [1998] 1 FLR 392*
- *Re D (A Child) [2014] EWCA Civ 315*
- *Re D [2018] EWFC B 64*
- *Re F (A Minor) (Blood Tests) [1993] 1 FLR 598*
- *Re F (In Utero) [1998] Fam 122*
- *Re G (Care: Challenge to Local Authority's Decision) [2003] 2 FLR 42*
- *Re G [2006] UKHL 43*
- *Re G (A Minor) (Parental Responsibility Order) [1994] 1 FLR 504*
- *Re (G) v Nottingham City Council [2008] EWHC 152 (Admin)*

- *Re (G) v Southwark LBC [2009] UKHL 26*
- *Re H (Minors) (Local Authority: Parental Rights) (No 3) [1991] 2 WLR 763*
- *Re H C (Parental Alienation) [2019] EWHC 2723 (Fam)*
- *Re KP (A Child) [2014] EWCA Civ 554, [2014] 1 WLR 4326*
- *Re L (Care: Threshold Criteria) [2007] 1 FLR 2050*
- *Re N (Children) (Adoption: Jurisdiction) [2015] EWCA Civ 1112*
- *Re NL (A Child) (Appeal: Interim Care Order: Facts and Reasons) [2014] EWHC 270 (Fam)*
- *Re O (A Child) (Supervision Order: Future Harm) [2001] EWCA Civ 16*
- *Re P (Terminating Parental Responsibility) [1995] 1 FLR 1048*
- *Re R [2005] EWCA Civ 1128*
- *Re R (A Child) [2014] EWCA Civ 1625*
- *Re S (A Child) [2014] EWCC B44 (Fam)*
- *Re S (Transfer of Residence) [2010] 1 FLR 1785*
- *Re S (Children) (Specific Issue Order: Religion: Circumcision) [2004] EWHC 1282 (Fam); [2005] 1 FLR 236; [2004] Fam Law 869*
- *Re X (Emergency Protection Orders) [2006] EWHC 510 (Fam)*
- *Re W (Children) [2012] EWCA 999*
- *Re Z (Child: Independent Social Work Assessments) [2014] EWHC 729 (Fam)*
- *Surrey County Council v M, F & E [2012] EWHC 2400*
- *Tyrer v United Kingdom [1978] 2 EHRR 1, [1978] ECHR 20*
- *W (A Child) [2016] EWCA Civ 793*
- *Williams and Another v LB Hackney [2018] UKSC 37*
- *Worcestershire County Council v AA [2019] EWHC 1855 (Fam)*
- *X Council v B (Emergency Protection Orders) [2004] EWHC 2015 (Fam); [2005] 1 FLR 34*
- *Yousef v Netherlands (Application no. 33711/96) 2002*
- *Z v Y [2019] EWHC 2255 (Fam)*

Reports

- *Building a Safe and Confident Future: Implementing the recommendations of the Social Work Task Force*, HM Government, 2010
- *Every Child Matters Green Paper*, HM Government, 2003

- *Family Justice Review Final Report*, November 2011
- *Haringey Local Safeguarding Children Board: Second Serious Case Review – Child A*, March 2009
- *Making not Breaking: Building relationships for our most vulnerable children, findings and recommendations of the Care Inquiry 2013*, Care Inquiry
- *Multi Agency Public Protection Arrangements Annual Report*, 2018/2019
- *People like Us: The Report of the Review of Safeguards for Children Living Away from Home*, Sir William Utting, August 1997
- *Report of the Inquiry into Child Abuse in Cleveland 1988*, Lady Justice Elizabeth Butler-Sloss
- *Residential Care in England: Report of Sir Martin Narey's independent review of children's residential care,* Sir Martin Narey, 2016
- *The Munro Review of Child Protection – Part One: A systems analysis*, DfE, 2010
- *The Munro Review of Child Protection, Interim Report: The child's journey*, DfE, 2011
- *The Protection of Children in England: A Progress Report*, DCSF, 2010
- *The Victoria Climbié Inquiry: Report of an Inquiry by Lord Laming*, 2003

Books/articles

- ADCS (2015) *Age Assessment Guidance: Guidance to assist social workers and their managers in undertaking age assessments in England*, London: ADCS
- Brown R and Ward H (2012) *Decision-Making within a Child's Timeframe: An overview of current research evidence for family justice professionals concerning child development and the impact of maltreatment*, Working Paper 16, London: Childhood Wellbeing Research Centre
- Department for Education (2010) *IRO Handbook*, London: DfE
- Family Justice Council (2010) *Guidelines for Judges Meeting Children who are subject to Family Proceedings*, available at: https://bit.ly/2PoZOe0
- Family Rights Group (2017) *Initial Family and Friends Care Assessment: A good practice guide*, available at: https://bit.ly/3fD3cN3
- Fauth R, Jelicic H, Hart D, Burton S, Shemmings D, Bergeron C, White K and Morris M (2010) *Effective Practice to Protect Children Living in 'Highly Resistant' Families: Safeguarding*, Knowledge Review 1, London: Centre for Excellence and Outcomes in Children and Young People's Services

- Ferguson L (2013) 'Not merely rights for children but children's rights: the theory gap and the assumption of the importance of children's rights', *International Journal of Children's Rights*, 21:2, pp 178–208
- Freeman M (2007) 'Why it remains important to take children's rights seriously', *International Journal of Children's Rights*, 15:1, pp 5–23
- Fortin J (2009) *Children's Rights and the Developing Law*, Cambridge: Cambridge University Press
- Home Office (2013) *New Government Domestic Violence and Abuse Definition*, available at: https://bit.ly/3gHk0n2
- Horn P (1997a) *The Victorian Country Child*, Stroud: Sutton Publishing
- Horn P (1997b) *The Victorian Town Child*, New York, NY: NYU Press
- MAPPA (2019) *MAPPA Guidance 2012* (version 4.5), available at: https://bit.ly/33ueHne
- McKay M (1994) 'The link between domestic violence and child abuse: assessment and treatment considerations', *Child Welfare*, 73:1
- Ministry for Housing, Communities and Local Government and DfE (2018) *Prevention of Homelessness and Provision of Accommodation for 16 and 17 Year Old Young People who may be Homeless and/or require Accommodation*, available at: https://bit.ly/3gCloY1
- Pritchard C and Williams R (2009) 'Comparing possible "child-abuse-related-deaths" in England and Wales with the major developed countries 1974–2006: signs of progress?' *British Journal of Social Work*, 40:6, pp 1700–1718
- Public Law Working Group (2020) *Recommendations to Achieve Best Practice in the Child Protection and Family Justice Systems: Special guardianship orders*, available at: https://bit.ly/3fwSIUL
- Solnit A, Freud A and Goldstein J (1973) *Beyond the Best Interests of the Child*, London: Free Press
- Turnell A (in press) *Building Safety in Child Protection Practice: Working with a strengths and solution focus in an environment of risk*, New York, NY: Palgrave

Glossary

ACPC	Area Child Protection Committees
ADCS	Association of Directors of Children's Services
ADM	Agency Decision-Maker
ASGLB	Adoption and Special Guardianship Leadership Board
ASF	Adoption Support Fund
CAFCASS	Children and Family Court Advisory Support Service
CAMHS	Community and Adolescent Mental Health Service
CAO	Child arrangements order
CLA	Child looked after, formerly referred to as looked after child (LAC)
CPC	Child Protection Conference
CPS	Crown Prosecution Service
DBS	Disclosure and Barring Service
DfE	Department for Education
ECHR	European Convention for the Protection of Human Rights and Fundamental Freedoms
FCA	Family Court Adviser, appointed from CAFCASS in private law proceedings
FDAC	Family Drug and Alcohol Court
FGC	Family Group Conference
FJC	Family Justice Council
FRG	Family Rights Group
GDPR	General Data Protection Regulation
ICO	Interim care order
IDVA	Independent Domestic Violence Advocate
IRO	Independent Reviewing Officer
LA	Local authority
LAC	Looked after child, now replaced by CLA
LFJB	Local Family Justice Board
LGO	Local Government Ombudsman
LSCB	Local Safeguarding Children Board
MAPPA	Multi-Agency Public Protection Arrangements.
MARAC	Multi-Agency Risk Assessment Conference
MASH	Multi-Agency Safeguarding Hub

MIAM	Mediation Information and Assessment Meeting
NASS	National Asylum Support Scheme
NMS	National Minimum Standards
OS	Official Solicitor
PLO	Public Law Outline
PA	Personal Adviser
PR	Parental responsibility
SG	Special guardian
SCR	Serious case review
SGO	Special guardianship order
SO	Supervision order
SW	Social worker
SWET	Social Work Evidence Template
UASC	Unaccompanied asylum-seeking child
UNCRC	United Nations Convention on the Rights of the Child

Appendix 1:
The Assessment Framework

Assessment Framework

(Reproduced from: Department of Health (2000) *Assessing Children in Need and their Families*, available at: https://bit.ly/2DfDHUS)

Appendix 2: Action following a strategy discussion

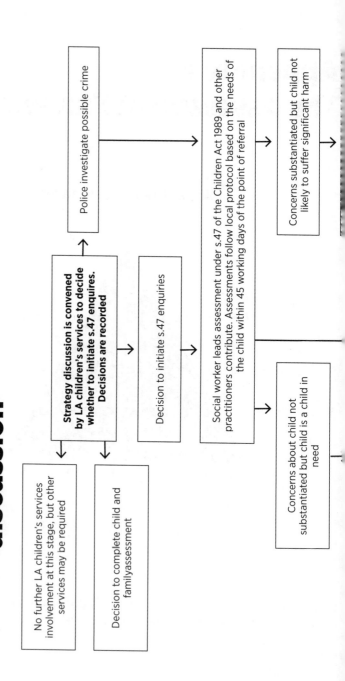

No further LA children's services involvement at this stage, but other services may be required

Decision to complete child and family assessment

Strategy discussion is convened by LA children's services to decide whether to initiate s.47 enquires. Decisions are recorded

Decision to initiate s.47 enquiries

Police investigate possible crime

Social worker leads assessment under s.47 of the Children Act 1989 and other practitioners contribute. Assessments follow local protocol based on the needs of the child within 45 working days of the point of referral

Concerns about child not substantiated but child is a child in need

Concerns substantiated but child not likely to suffer significant harm

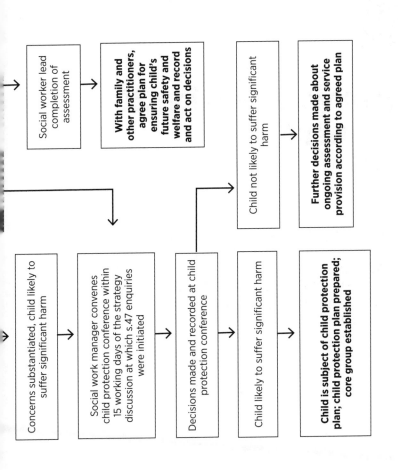

Social worker lead completion of assessment

With family and other practitioners, agree plan for ensuring child's future safety and welfare and record and act on decisions

Child not likely to suffer significant harm

Further decisions made about ongoing assessment and service provision according to agreed plan

Concerns substantiated, child likely to suffer significant harm

Social work manager convenes child protection conference within 15 working days of the strategy discussion at which s.47 enquiries were initiated

Decisions made and recorded at child protection conference

Child likely to suffer significant harm

Child is subject of child protection plan; child protection plan prepared; core group established

(Reproduced: from HM Government (2018) *Working Together to Safeguard Children*, London: HM Government)

Appendix 3: Section 20 agreement

AGREEMENT BETWEEN [LOCAL AUTHORITY] AND
[PERSONS WITH PARENTAL RESPONSIBILITY]
FOR THE ACCOMMODATION UNDER SECTION 20
OF THE CHILDREN ACT 1989/SECTION 76 OF THE
SOCIAL SERVICES AND WELL-BEING (WALES) ACT
2014 OF [CHILDREN]

THE RELEVANT PERSONS

The children: [names]

The persons with parental responsibility: [names]

The local authority: [name]

Date: [date]

Agreement

- This is an agreement between [local authority] and [persons with parental responsibility].

- The agreement is that [children] will be placed in [say, foster care] by [local authority].

- In legal terms, that placement is happening under [sub-section of section 20 of the 1989 Act].

The placement and the children's wishes

- The purpose of that placement is [purpose]. The current plan is that [current plan for children's return home] and that the [children] will remain accommodated by the local authority for a period of [X weeks/months].

- It [has/has not] been possible to find out the [children's] wishes and feelings. [The children's] wishes and feelings are [wishes and feelings].

Agreement of the persons with parental responsibility and right to remove

- [The person with parental responsibility] does not at the moment object to [the children] being placed in [say, foster care].

- [The person with parental responsibility] may at any time remove [the children] from [say, foster care].

- [The person with parental responsibility] [has/has not] had legal advice.

Reviews

- [This is/this is not] an agreement for the accommodation of a newborn baby or child under six months. In the event that it is an agreement for the accommodation of a newborn baby or child under six months, the exceptional circumstances requiring the use of s.20/s.76 are [exceptional circumstances].

- [The local authority] intends to review this placement every [X weeks] and the persons with parental responsibility will, after each review, be updated by the local authority on its plan moving forward.

SIGNATURES

Signature:

- Signed and dated:
    - [The persons with parental responsibility]
    - [Local authority]

Where required to be translated into a foreign language:

- This document has been written in English and translated into [foreign language]. The [person with parental responsibility] has read it in [foreign language].

  - Signed and dated in [foreign language]: ["I have read this document and agree to its terms"].

  - Signed and dated by [named interpreter].

Where an advocate or intermediary has assisted

- The [person with parental responsibility] has been assisted by [name; advocate/intermediary].

- I [advocate/intermediary] confirm that I have read this document with and explained it to [person with parental responsibility] and I am satisfied that the [person with parental responsibility] understands its contents.

- [Signed and dated by advocate/intermediary].

Checklist for local authority

- Are you satisfied that the persons with parental responsibility have capacity to consent?

- Are you satisfied that the persons with parental responsibility have consented?

- If the persons with parental responsibility are not native English speakers, has the agreement been translated into their native language?

(Reproduced with permission from Public Law Working Group (2019) *Recommendations to Achieve Best Practice in the Child Protection and Family Justice Systems*, pp 248–252)

Appendix 4:
Public Law Outline 2014 (26 weeks)

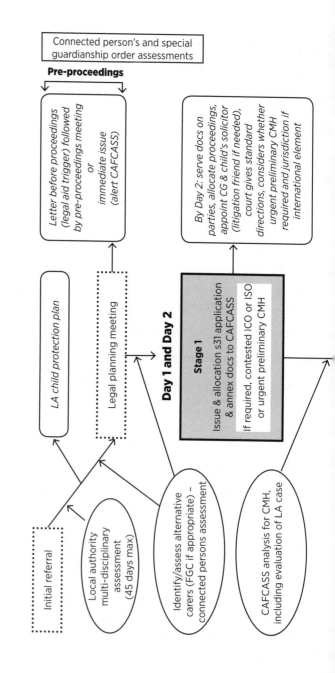

Connected person's and special guardianship order assessments

Pre-proceedings

Letter before proceedings (legal aid trigger) followed by pre-proceedings meeting
or
immediate issue (alert CAFCASS)

By Day 2: serve docs on parties, allocate proceedings, appoint CG & child's solicitor (litigation friend if needed), court gives standard directions, considers whether urgent preliminary CMH required and jurisdiction if international element

LA child protection plan

Legal planning meeting

Day 1 and Day 2

Stage 1
Issue & allocation s31 application & annex docs to CAFCASS

If required, contested ICO or ISO or urgent preliminary CMH

Initial referral

Local authority multi-disciplinary assessment (45 days max)

Identify/assess alternative carers (FGC if appropriate) – connected persons assessment

CAFCASS analysis for CMH, including evaluation of LA case

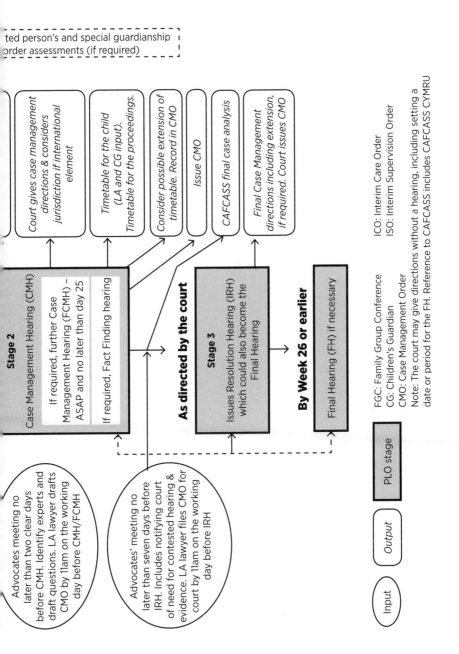

ted person's and special guardianship order assessments (if required)

Stage 2
Case Management Hearing (CMH)

If required, further Case Management Hearing (FCMH) – ASAP and no later than day 25

If required, Fact Finding hearing

Court gives case management directions & considers jurisdiction if international element

Timetable for the child (LA and CG input). Timetable for the proceedings.

Consider possible extension of timetable. Record in CMO

Issue CMO

CAFCASS final case analysis

Final Case Management directions including extension, if required. Court issues CMO

As directed by the court

Stage 3
Issues Resolution Hearing (IRH) which could also become the Final Hearing

By Week 26 or earlier
Final Hearing (FH) if necessary

Advocates meeting no later than two clear days before CMH. Identify experts and draft questions. LA lawyer drafts CMO by 11am on the working day before CMH/FCMH

Advocates' meeting no later than seven days before IRH. Includes notifying court of need for contested hearing & evidence. LA lawyer files CMO for court by 11am on the working day before IRH

FGC: Family Group Conference
CG: Children's Guardian
CMO: Case Management Order
Note: The court may give directions without a hearing, including setting a date or period for the FH. Reference to CAFCASS includes CAFCASS CYMRU

ICO: Interim Care Order
ISO: Interim Supervision Order

PLO stage

Output

Input

235